What the Bleep Is Going On Here?

OTHER BOOKS BY RAFE MAIR

Rafe Mair

What the Bleep Is Going On Here?

With a foreword by Gordon Gibson

HARBOUR PUBLISHING

Harbour Publishing Co. Ltd
P.O. Box 219, Madeira Park, BC, V0N 2H0
www.harbourpublishing.com

Edited by Betty Keller. Cover design by Anna Comfort.
Some of the essays in this collection were previously published in whole or in part in *The Tyee*, http://thetyee.ca.
The excerpt beginning on page 141 is reprinted from the journal *Finest Hour*, No. 117, Winter 2002–03, by permission of the Churchill Centre.
Printed in Canada on 100% recycled paper.

Harbour Publishing acknowledges financial support from the Government of Canada through the Book Publishing Industry Development Program and the Canada Council for the Arts, and from the Province of British Columbia through the BC Arts Council and the Book Publishing Tax Credit.

THE CANADA COUNCIL | LE CONSEIL DES ARTS
FOR THE ARTS | DU CANADA
SINCE 1957 | DEPUIS 1957

BRITISH
COLUMBIA
ARTS COUNCIL
Supported by the Province of British Columbia

Library and Archives Canada Cataloguing in Publication

Mair, Rafe, 1931–
        What the bleep is going on here? / Rafe Mair.

ISBN 978-1-55017-458-8

        I. Title.

AC8.M315 2008   081   C2008-900010-2

Contents

*For the Venerable Louis Rivers—Lou—
the man who has treated Wendy and me, his parish
heretics, with so much understanding and love, and for
Georgie, his inspiration and so often ours, this book is
humbly dedicated.*

Foreword

My old friend Rafe Mair has done it again—another highly readable book that will entertain and inform in equal parts for most of us and send not a few of his targets to their publicists and lawyers screaming "What can be done?"

He tackles the environment first, asking if global warming is real and importantly, caused by humans (he thinks so; I favour the sun), and goes on to wonder why British Columbians are killing Magellanic Penguins, an answer you will have to gain for yourself.

Fish farms are here of course, out of a very deep personal concern. Unending human demand for meat ended the time of the buffalo in North America very quickly (responsibly managed cattle ranches came too late) and we are doing the same to the sea.

World affairs capture his attention, from scorching portraits of leaders like Bush and Putin to a usefully provocative and sympathetic approach to Palestine.

As always with Rafe, his encyclopaedic knowledge of politics and the law takes the reader on a jolly good tour of our democratic system, from the powerless MP to the foolish secrecy of budgets, and from the impartiality of judges to the need for (or not) of Quebec.

The personalities of the famous get a fair share of attention, some of it with the surprising sympathy afforded by the perspective of one who has "been there and met that." More than a few names are dropped, but they are ones worth picking up in the first place.

While the book has the highly accessible facility to be read in short bites as it is in form a collection of essays, the whole is something much more than that. Anyone who knows Rafe Mair knows of his fierce dedication to freedom, to common sense, to telling it like it is, and to the good of the ordinary person.

So the enduring themes of due process, good science, honesty and sound institutions unite the whole. When the movers and shakers meet these tests, they get a thumbs up. When not, they get speared by a powerful pen.

There is a great deal to learn here—the stories themselves in the foreground, of course, but always within that background of aiming for a better country and world, which shines through as the unifying framework. You may agree with Rafe on this and that or disagree with him, but it is hard not to love him (and read him!) for seeking the public good.

—Gordon Gibson
Former leader of the Liberal Party of BC,
senior fellow of the Fraser Institute,
political commentator and author

Preface

This book contains a couple of articles I've written and adjusted, some thoughts I've put on my website, which—if the numbers are correct—will not have been read by most of you, and some new musings. Quite often these musings will have grown out of previous published and unpublished thoughts. As Emerson said, "A foolish consistency is the hobgoblin of little minds," and I take that to heart and try to re-examine my thoughts based upon new experiences and events.

I hope some of this book gets you laughing with me and at me, that it makes you happy in agreement and angry as hell in disagreement. My main hope is that you enjoy it and find it worthy of the paltry sum it demands at your bookstore.

Like other books I've written, most of the chapters speak for themselves so you might find that the table in the loo is the place to leave this one. To read, of course!

PART I

Global Alarms

A General View of the Environment

Thank God, it's finally over—or is it? The blockbuster environmental report put out by a UN-sponsored blue ribbon panel of scientists in late 2006 permits no argument about global warming except that of a fool. The results of increasing greenhouse gases will be very serious even if we start doing something now—and catastrophic if we don't. In fact, the most important message from this report is that the dramatic consequences we once just feared for the future are already with us and worsening by the day.

What a criminal shame. What horrible governmental neglect—and deliberate neglect at that! In the years we should have been learning and acting, our governments permitted and even encouraged the horrible practices that now threaten the very existence of our own species on this planet. This shameful time, the fifty-year period since Rachel Carson wrote *Silent Spring*, are as Churchill would likely have called them "the years the locusts ate."

I'm not an aboriginal person, but I share many of their values. First Nations people approach the environment from a point of view that is both spiritual and conservationist. Their spiritual or, if you will, moral arguments, are deeply compelling, though we pay them little mind, but I believe that, if there were no other arguments, the moral compulsion that we must repair and revitalize our earth trumps all other considerations. I have fought for the preservation of our wild salmon for years. In government I fought in support of a doughty band of private citizens to save the beautiful Skagit River from the ravages of a hydroelectric dam. (Interestingly, BC Hydro, which opposed my position on the Skagit, attended a Social Credit caucus with pictures of the Skagit that made it look like a moonscape. What they didn't say until I embarrassed them was that these pictures were of the Skagit on the *American* side of the border!) I fought alongside allies from every walk of life to eliminate the right of Alcan to even further reduce the Nechako River and thus place runs of sockeye and tyee under a death sentence. I fought under the leadership of the gutsy group called PRAWN to save the Upper Pitt River system from a gravel-pit operation that would have wreaked grave and perhaps terminal damage. I have fought with all my strength to support the courageous Alexandra Morton in her battle to save Broughton Archipelago pink and chum salmon runs from destruction by Atlantic-salmon fish cages and the millions of sea lice they host.

In all these cases the real work has been done by British Columbian women and men of all races for no personal gain. They do it because it is right. It's an obligation on all British Columbians, indeed all people. But there's more to it than that. Man is charged with the responsibility to leave the environment as he found it and, in our case, to restore and enhance that which has been harmed. Every living creature is in our care and every species that becomes extinct is a mark of shame against our names.

Governments have abandoned their responsibilities and industry only accepts morality if it doesn't cost them anything and only obeys laws when they are compelled. Because industry's raison d'être is to make money for shareholders, it has become the general rule that the more a company boasts of what they are doing to save the environment, the bigger the eco-rapists they likely are.

If you think that is cynical, hearken back to Alcan's recent ad campaign, which portrays the company as the saviour of our environment. Can you imagine Alcan of all companies claiming to be "green"? This only demonstrates that the "big lie" technique is still alive and well! The skills of the PR artist know no bounds or sense of decency. Governments, on the other hand, cannot see past this year's budget and the next election day. This leaves us, Canada's citizenry, entirely responsible. Unfortunately, Pogo, that bashful hero of a comic strip sadly gone, had it dead-on when he said, "We have met the enemy and he is us." It is we who buy from the fish farmers and other evil despoilers of our planet. It is we who elect the political handmaidens of those despoilers. But we can refuse to support rapacious industry and we can refuse to vote for lousy politicians.

It's been interesting to me, a long-time environmentalist, to see both the federal and the provincial governments go from as black as the inside of a goat to racing green in about the space of ten days in early 2007. When you consider that during the leadership debates of early 2006 there was not one question asked about the environment and by the end of that year all major political parties, both federal and provincial, were falling all over themselves to "out-green" one another, we really have seen a Damascus-like conversion. The trouble is that Prime Minister Harper is obviously in the "environment game" for the political chips, and opposition leader Stéphane Dion's rhetoric is substantially more robust than his plan. Some of the expected boo-birds have risen from the ashes to say things like, "We can't afford Kyoto," the implication being that this means we're off the hook for doing anything. This is a bit like a homeowner refusing to pay his fire insurance in order to save money even though a forest fire is moving slowly but inexorably towards him. Not being able to afford to deal with the environment is just not on.

This is not to say that there will be no financial challenges ahead if we are to save this planet. We must expect higher taxes on gasoline for one thing. There should be tax incentives for those who drive smaller, more fuel-efficient vehicles, while SUVs and pickups ought to be charged a surtax. (The NDP started this but they neglected to give an exemption to farmers and ranchers, which is doable and fair.) But what I fear will happen is that, while dealing with global warming, senior governments and perhaps local governments as well will turn a blind eye to other environmental problems such as fish farms, sewage treatment and industrial waste. Might not a government now say to a mill, "If you reduce your emissions, we will relax the rules on discharging waste into rivers and oceans?"

It's true that, because we didn't do our duty from the beginning, the catch-up is too much to handle in as timely a fashion as we might like. But that is no excuse for not getting started in a substantial way nor is it an excuse to permit or encourage other environmental degradation. Unfortunately, it is a common human trait to make perfection the enemy of improvement, and this tendency is now well at play in the environmental field. We can't do Kyoto, it is said, because it is just not possible to achieve the standards that Kyoto set. Moreover, they say, as long as the US and China won't honour Kyoto, why should we? These are the cries of those who need new arguments against doing anything. In a sense, they are posting a suicide note: *I can't live forever so I'm not going to try to stay healthy.*

Of course, it's true that Canada can't bring itself up the standard we might have reached had we started on time. This country was one of the first to sign the Kyoto Protocol, on April 29, 1998, but formal ratification didn't come until more than four years later (December 17, 2002). It's also true to say that the atmosphere cannot be saved—if it can be saved now at all—without the participation of China and the US. But that can't stop us, surely, from doing what we should, by doing our part. It is the obligation of the entire world to save the planet, but because some countries won't accept their share of responsibility—or any share at all—it is all the more important that our country leads by example. Canada can do more to convince other countries to participate, of course. It can keep up the pressure during trade talks, through the UN, and by one-on-one diplomacy. But it's going to be a hell of a tough sell. Politicians don't like to make any financial commitment past the current fiscal year, and even if they can force themselves to make an exception, they don't want to spend money if the public approval that it buys won't come until decades after they've left office.

But we must press on. If we take the lead, others may follow. If they don't, catastrophe is certain. Canadians will, of course, be forced to share that catastrophe but at least we'll know, as a justifiable boost to national pride, that we tried. And even if we just take on what can be done, it will be a good start, a valuable morale builder and will set a good example for others. Wars lost on paper can be won in fact, as proved by the British under Winston Churchill in 1945; if you want to win badly enough, you can surmount the heavy odds against you.

But why, you ask, am I giving you yet another lecture about the environment? For one thing, the arguments must be marshalled. The pollyannas, often with dated, unreliable and unrelated credentials, need only say, "Fear not! All is well!" and thus have a totally undeserved impact just because to believe them makes us feel better. My experience of this syndrome comes out of the fight against Atlantic salmon fish farms, where industry and their hired governments have argued that all the science supports their policies whereas the truth is that all the independent, peer-reviewed published evidence (and yes, I said ALL) is firmly to the contrary. Independent science (that is, science unsullied by government and industry) peer-reviewed and published, paints a very grim picture on every environmental front and has been ignored or pooh-poohed by industry and government flacks. In fact, the tactics of industry and government in the environmental field eerily resemble—indeed replicate—those refined and perfected by the tobacco industry, which proves that people will believe the "big lie" if it is comforting and is repeated often enough by flacks and the captive "experts" in lab coats who appear on your television screen. Fifty-nine years after the Surgeon General of the United States declared the clear connection between tobacco and cancer, and in spite of the mountains of evidence supporting the Surgeon General's findings, the tobacco companies are still very much in the fight. They have denied responsibility from day one. If you question the evidence and deny that much damage has been done by their industry, simply look at the statistics, especially from outside North America. The advertising that the tobacco companies piously say they would never use in Canada is standard stuff in Third World countries. The industry has lied from the beginning about their marketing strategies, especially with regard to seducing the young. They have now reached the point—get this!—where they are so confident in their position that they offer seminars on how to quit smoking! Overall, the tobacco death dealers are now doing better than ever, and tobacco farmers are still getting agricultural subsidies from Canada and the US.

The tobacco industry provides us with a clear example of how industry defends its environmentally rapacious and unhealthy actions and policies and provides a template for governments. Thus, I proceed on the assumption that industry and government, dealing with environmental matters, lie through their teeth and are never to be trusted.

I make no pretence of presenting either industry's or government's case. They do that very well through huge expenditures of your money—whether you are a consumer or a taxpayer or both. PR people for industry and government are well paid to spin their client's propaganda and are accountable only to themselves.

Believe me, Kyoto is a problem. Even if we had started on time, it's doubtful that we could have met its guidelines. But we surely must start.

Is Global Warming for Real?

In early 2007, Bryan Zandberg, an environmental writer with a regular column in thetyee.ca, interviewed Professor William Rees from the School of Community and Regional Planning (SCARP) at UBC, where he has taught since 1969. Said Dr. Rees, "This year is the first time in tens of thousands of years you could take a kayak to the North Pole. That's the evidence, so don't give me the optimism about technology moving us forward because it isn't." In the same story James Lovelock, the man who wrote *The Revenge of Gaia*, said, "There's nothing to stop the earth from slouching towards a 'coma' now taking billions of us . . . along with her." And Dr. Daniel Pauly, director of the Fisheries Centre at UBC and an outspoken critic of fish farms, related that in view of the situation he sometimes has trouble getting out of bed in the morning! *Time* magazine has ranked Dr. Pauly in the top fifty world scientists. If you didn't read Bryan Zandberg's article, do so!

I thought it might be interesting to see how Patrick Moore, the Greenpeacer-turned-industry mouthpiece, would respond to Mr. Zandberg's article so I emailed him a copy. Here's what he had to say:

"The fact is we don't have a crystal ball and the future can't be predicted with certainty...If [the environmental situation] is really that bad and irreversible, the logical thing to do is *party*..." Unhappily, Moore represents the feeling of most of the corporate community. Either it isn't happening and the mass of the scientific community is wrong or, if it they are right, there's nothing we can do, so let's all go out and get pissed!

I'm six years past my Biblical allotment and I worry myself sick about this planet, in part for my eight grandchildren, but even more from a philosophical or, if you will, moral point of view. Don't we have a moral obligation to leave this earth in better shape than we found it? Does it not go further, much further than just saving fuel costs by more efficiency? Must we not insist that all those in power—be it a municipal councillor, a union leader, a captain of industry, a cabinet minister, a premier, a prime minister or a president of a powerful country—make every effort to make dramatic changes for the better starting NOW?

If we insist upon allowing our natural yearning for good news to cloud our judgment so that we accept the sort of dangerous nonsense Patrick Moore and the PR companies spew, it's all over. It's the death sentence, a particularly horrible one because its implementation is slow. And though we commit the murder, it is our children and grandchildren who will suffer the penalty imposed.

It moves one—me anyway—to tears of sadness and frustration.

Why Are British Columbians Killing Magellanic Penguins?

L et me pose an environmental question that no government has dared ask the fish farm industry: "What is the connection between farmed salmon and the Magellanic penguin?"

The answer demands a bit of background and one fundamental fact—Atlantic salmon must eat. Farmers know that and have found that anchovies—from someone else's waters, of course—work nicely to keep their charges happy. It is, to the farmers and our governments, irrelevant that it takes five to seven kilograms of fish like anchovy to make the feed necessary to produce one kilogram of farmed salmon. (Dr. David Suzuki has been asking in vain for many years why they are allowed to do this. It clearly makes no sense and on its own should be a reason to clear out Atlantic-salmon fish farms.)

Anchovies are found in scattered areas throughout the world's oceans, but they are concentrated in temperate waters, such as the Mediterranean and the coasts of South America, and are rare or absent in very cold waters, such as the North Pacific. In recent years they have been fished to a highly dangerous level off the Peruvian and Chilean coast and now the fish farmers are turning more and more to Argentina. In January 2007, *Science* magazine stated that Atlantic anchovies (*Engraulis anchoita*) found on the Patagonia coast are a crucial part of the southwest Atlantic ecosystem. In the food chain they are ranked just above plankton and they sustain a wide range of animals of the Patagonian shelf. They alone provide for more than half of a Magellanic penguin's diet.

Recently anchovies have become an important ingredient in the fish meal used to feed commercially farmed fish. The article suggests that as the human population increases so will the demand for food produced by global aquaculture. Although anchovy populations naturally fluctuate, overfishing to satisfy the increasing need for fish meal will place the entire Atlantic ecosystem at risk.

There are three important points to be made here.

First, the anchovy population is critical to many species in the region's ecosystem. Second, though we tend to look upon farming Atlantic salmon only in terms of our own environment, the fish farmer's footprint actually pops up halfway around the world. Thus, as we move to save our wild salmon from execution by fish cages, we're helping to save a lot of critters who live a long way away. And, third, when you eat that farmed salmon, remember that you're munching on anchovies that should be in the beaks of those Magellanic penguins.

As long as our environmental attention is keyed in on Kyoto to the exclusion of all else, the ongoing despoilers of our environment will pollute away and seldom, if ever, be called to account. And until enough of us understand this, fish farmers and other abusers of the environment will not be dealt with.

It comes as no surprise to those of us who follow these things that a recent study under the leadership of Dr. Boris Worm of Dalhousie, published in *Science*, predicts the collapse of the world's fish stocks by 2048; as far back as 1998 UBC's Dr. Daniel Pauly has been making similar predictions. And in last February's *Science* it was reported that 90 percent of the oceans' large predators are gone.

We are the problem and we must be the solution. For, calamitous though these findings are, there's hope if we don't lose sight of our objective, if we work like hell and make sacrifices. This is particularly true for BC since we are one of the few faint hopes for recovery and maintenance of fish stocks. And how ironic it is that fish farms in the Broughton Archipelago made exactly this point: For the one year that a migration path in the Broughton Archipelago was free of fish farms, there were excellent returns of pink and chum salmon in that area. Let me quote from Dr. John Volpe, the renowned fish biologist from the University of Victoria, who's been involved in many studies of BC's plague of fish farms: "The independent scientific community speaks with a single voice with regards to sea lice and their impact on wild salmon. Salmon farms kill wild salmon. There's no debate around that. It's been known and acknowledged in Europe for more than a decade." In September 2007, a letter signed by eighteen scientists was sent to both Prime Minister Harper and Premier Campbell, telling these first ministers that their policy has been dead wrong. With the arrogance we've come to expect, Premier Campbell and Prime Minister Harper have ignored this letter. The lesson, clear and obvious as it is, has not yet sunk in with the governments. They're in denial since their concern is with helping their political supporters make money, and to do that, you can't trouble yourself with environmental matters!

Interestingly but sadly lost in the debates that have centred around the predation by sea lice on migrating fish is the fact that almost no one opposes aquaculture per se. What is opposed by so many of us is the siting of these farms in the migration path of wild salmon smolts. I invite you to think about that. However attractive the river mouth may be to fish farmers, if you had the power, would you let them put these lousy (literally) fish farms in the path of young salmon on their migration exercise? Of course not, but that is precisely what the owners, with the encouragement of the politicians, have done *and want to continue to do.*

Our sins go back a long way. As kids we were told to "throw the little ones back" and indeed that philosophy is still the law. Think about that. Throwing the little fish back has two main problems—unlike its bigger brother/sister it probably won't survive its return, usually bleeding, to the ocean and if it does, it must now set out on its journey full of the dangers that its big brother/sister has survived. Meanwhile, the big fish you catch has survived all manner of problems and is now big enough to spawn. Kill him/her and you kill a solution to the diminished fish problem. Commercial fishermen will always take the large fish because it brings in the most money or for the recreational fisherman the bragging rights. Thus they destroy that which is about to mate. The large fish gone, the prey get smaller and smaller. Then comes the wipeout.

The idiocy of governments, indeed the mindset of governments along with their corporate handmaidens, has played a huge role in this. They have permitted fishing without having the faintest idea of the fish's lifespan or breeding habits. Thus many species are dying out because commercial fishermen, seeking the largest fish, have all but wiped out entire species not realizing that these fish may not breed for ten to twenty years, meaning their preferred catch is all that stands between survival and extinction. One need only look to eastern Canada to see how governments, industry and unions conspired to turn a blind eye to overfishing and thus the imminent extinction of the cod. The Australasian fish the John Dory and orange roughy have been nearly exterminated by commercial fishing because it was not understood that both these fish are very long-lived, thus the preferred catches were eliminating the spawners.

Very few escape blame for this situation though each one at fault says someone else is worse. But here are the mug shots: The citizen who doesn't care, the politician, the fishing company, the worker and, especially, his union. The voters have yet to visit a single political consequence on the politician who, under no real political pressure from the public, does worse than nothing—in fact, actually contributes to the problem. The salmon farming companies (all from outside BC) only care about their shareholders, including their executives with big salaries and, often, huge bunches of share options. Unions aren't much better as they put jobs first whether in the fish farm industry or the wild fishery (and how's that for a conflict of interest?) and even insist that fisheries remain open when there's nothing left to catch.

(In 1979 I attended an international fish conference where representatives from the United States and from Canada divided up the allowable fishery on "ground" fish, allowing themselves to catch more fish than existed!) Meanwhile, the drift nets and long lines of Japan and South Korea have wreaked havoc not only on the targeted fish but on the by-kill—that which was not sought yet was captured.

It's interesting to note, in passing, that while fish farmers and the governments reject the huge quantity of scientific evidence that tells the consequences of badly sited fish farms, they enthusiastically, dare I say ghoulishly, greet the scientific evidence that the world's stock of fisheries is en route to extinction. The fewer wild fish the better because it means more money for fish farmers and the political parties they support. It's rather like the Vietnam War wisdom that said, "In order to save the village, we had to destroy it."

We in British Columbia must understand that, unlike most places, for us there's a ray of hope. While we're presently moving in the wrong direction, if we get our act together, we can get back on track, save and restore our wonderful Pacific salmon. Governments must move against anything man-controlled that will hurt our fishery, and the first thing they must do is legislate the "Precautionary Principle," which means that any application of any sort that may be injurious to any fishing on our coasts must demonstrate that it will do no harm, the emphasis being on "beyond a reasonable doubt." In other words, the onus is on industry, not the public, as it has been hitherto.

Next the Department of Fisheries and Oceans must have its

mandate to promote aquaculture removed and replaced by its traditional mandate to protect wild fish and to force those who would use our oceans to demonstrate beyond a reasonable doubt that they can do so safely. It is time to send government-shilling-for-industry back to the economic development ministries where it belongs.

Finally all British Columbians must understand that the very last thing we need as we go into recovery mode is an increase of fish farms in the paths of migrating salmon. All applications for the licensing of new fish farms must be denied along with the corollary that those farms now endangering wild salmon must be closed or removed.

These things we can do and these things we must do.

If you, like me, need a string on your finger to remind you of things, when you hear "fish farms" just think of those Magellanic penguins starving so that offshore companies can steal their food, rape our fishery then take their ill-gotten gains home.

PART II

This Warring World

As Ithers See Us

*O wad some Power the giftie gie us
to see oursels as ithers see us!*

— ROBERT BURNS

While some countries in the Middle East are contained within artificial boundaries, Persia, though known since 1935 as Iran, has been Persia for eons. But in 1908 oil was discovered there and soon thereafter Churchill, then First Lord of the Admiralty, switched the Royal Navy from coal to oil, thus instituting one hundred years of foreign intervention, first by the British, then the Russians and now the Americans. Consider for a moment these events through the eyes of an Iranian, whose civilization is one of the oldest in the world. As you sip your dark coffee in Tehran, wouldn't you regard the Europeans as enemies and the United States as the biggest of all? Wouldn't you recall how in 1953 the US and Britain toppled the elected government of Mohammad Mosaddeq and restored Mohammad Reza Shah to the Peacock throne? And how could you ignore the war with Iraq from September 1980 to August 1988, twice the length of World War I and with half a million Iranian deaths, a war where Saddam Hussein was supported by the United States? And now that the nuclear-armed Americans are on either side of your country in Iraq and Afghanistan, would you not demand of your government that they install nuclear weapons to meet nuclear weapons? Don't perceptions depend on where you sip your coffee?

I'd be the last person on earth to suggest that we need more members in the "nuclear club." But if I were an Iranian and looked around me and saw a nuclear-armed Pakistan, a nuclear-armed Russia, a nuclear-armed Israel and a nuclear-armed United States as my neighbours, I might think that the only way I could defend myself is to have these countries as terrified of me as I am of them.

To see oursels as ithers see us . . .

✳   #   ✳

The other day I had coffee (Turkish, which I love) with Ali Gazah, a Muslim originally from Palestine but now a student in Egypt. Here is the interview I did:

Q. Why can't Hamas accept the right of Israel to exist?

A. Easy. Until Israel recognizes our borders—pre-1967— they have not recognized us. When a settlement is reached, if it ever happens, we will, of course, as a nation recognize Israel.

Q. Why would Israel recognize Palestine when they suffer so many losses from, amongst other things, suicide bombers?

A. We made a serious mistake in targeting civilians and that will stop with Arafat gone. May I point out that Israel has killed five times as many Palestinians than we have Israelis, and if you die by a rocket or a suicide's bomb, the result is the same. But you must recognize—as Israeli governments have not—that official control over these matters is impossible. Moreover, we say that Israel has used these incidents to block the peace process.

Q. How is that?

A. Making negotiations subject to the absence of bombings makes the peace process hostage to any Palestinian with a bomb who doesn't want peace.

Q. How can you expect Israel or the United States to accept Hamas as the negotiating power?

A. The West is very selective in its morality. The United States, for example, even after Pearl Harbor, recognized the French collaborator Vichy government, which sent Jews by the thousands into death camps. The US also recognized the Soviet Union run by a madman who slaughtered literally millions of its citizens. It recognizes China, which has committed similar atrocities and on it goes. Most obviously, the United States and the UK have dealt with the IRA. Besides, the right wing element in Israel won't recognize our right to a national existence and say we should all move to Jordan. It's also important to know that we, who were in possession of Palestine for nearly two thousand years, didn't ask Jews to make it their national homeland.

Q. But the UN and the US recognized the new state of Israel in 1948.

A. Lord Balfour, with his famous pronouncement, had no business doing so. Britain didn't own Palestine but held it as a trust, a mandate from the League of Nations. As more Jews came we protested—even had a mini civil war in the late '30s—but who were we to stand up to the UK? Let me ask you a question. What right do these European countries have to meddle in other peoples' business? What right do the UK, France, the Russians and the Americans to tell us what we should do?

Q. Are you saying that European motives have not been to bring peace and democracy to Muslim countries?

A. (sputtering at this point) Democracy has nothing to do with it! The motive is oil! Ever since Winston Churchill converted the Royal Navy to oil before the First World War, the West, under the guise of bringing peace and democracy, have really been protecting their oil supply.

Q. But, like it or not, the world is dependent on oil.

A. That doesn't give anyone the right to march into places

that don't belong to them, preach crap about democracy, and take over our countries. When Saddam Hussein took over Kuwait, to the US and Britain that was a no-no, yet it's quite okay for the US and the UK to take over Iraq!

Q. But you have some terrible governments in the Muslim world.

A. We do. But what gives the United States the right to change these governments? And while we're on that subject, why don't the Americans invade Egypt, Syria and Saudi Arabia if they want to get rid of vicious dictators and impose their way of life on them? The answer is simple — Egypt and Saudia Arabia are ruthless dictatorships who are friendly to the US and there is no oil in Syria.

Q. What about Al Qaeda and 9/11?

A. I sympathize with all those people who were wounded or bereaved. But we're at war. Many of us view America as an enemy just as America regarded Germany and Italy as enemies. In wartime, innocent people get killed. But don't talk to me about terror. What was Hiroshima if not terror? Hiroshima was not a military centre and the bomb was dropped during the week in rush hour so as to kill the most civilians.

Q. But surely that was different. Then the enemies were wicked and they challenged the entire world.

A. Why do I have so much trouble convincing you that we see the United States as wicked?

Q. But isn't terror simply wrong when used by civilized people?

A. I agree. But what were Hiroshima and Nagasaki, Dresden and Hamburg, London and Coventry, Tokyo and Berlin if not terrorism? Terrorism is scaring people into demanding that their governments give up. When the West does it, it's okay but when we do it it's evil. In fact, it's all terrorism but with different explanations, depending on who's doing it.

Q. But what about Iran making nuclear weapons?

A. While any increase in nuclear weapons is bad and, for good reason, scary, how come Britain, the United States, Russia, China, India and Pakistan can have bombs and Iran can't? Besides, people tend to forget that the UN did its job by keeping Iraq free of weapons of mass destruction; the problem was that the US and Britain didn't accept UN findings. Let the UN Security Council deal with this.

Q. Finally, Ali, surely civilized countries must deal with the likes of Saddam Hussein, come to the rescue of downtrodden people, especially women? And must not the US, as the only superpower, be that rescuer?

A. No! The United Nations must be the rescuer. America's job is to start paying its dues to the UN, supporting it in every way whenever that support is sought. The United States and Britain have no right to tell any country how to govern itself. Moreover, these paragons of democratic virtue are highly selective of which dictatorships they will overthrow. The examples of repressive countries being avoided by the United States are many indeed, but let me leave you with this thought: Saudi Arabia is the personal fiefdom of a royal family that suppresses all dissent, keeps women in near slavery, flogs and imprisons victims of rape, stones adulterers, cuts off thieves' hands and acts as the banker for Al Qaeda. But instead of seeing the US bringing pressure for democracy in Saudi Arabia, we see pictures of the Crown Prince and George W. Bush holding hands! In fact, we see the US and UK as hypocritical meddlers who use high-flown rhetoric as an excuse to protect economic interests at the expense of the Middle East.

Ali Gazeh doesn't exist, of course. But if he did, would these questions and answers help us "see oursels as ithers see us"?

My Take on Israel Has Changed

The overriding problem in Israel/Palestine is that, for more than a quarter century the actions of some Israeli leaders have been in direct conflict with the official policies of the international community and their own negotiated agreements. Regardless of the fact that the Palestinians had no formalized state, they have had governments during that time, whether headed by Yasser Arafat or Mahmoud Abbas or one with Abbas as president and Hamas controlling the parliament and cabinet. (Given the constant lurching from left to right in Israel, it's a bit much to hear Israelis call Palestinians politically erratic.) But Israel's continued control and colonization of Palestinian land and money has been the primary obstacle to a comprehensive peace agreement in the Holy Land. And in order to perpetuate the occupation, Israeli forces have deprived their unwilling Palestinian citizens of basic human rights. No objective person could observe existing conditions in the West Bank and dispute these statements.

The bottom line was recently expressed in these words:

Peace will come to Israel and the Middle East only when the Israeli government is willing to comply with international law, with the Roadmap for Peace, with official American policy, with the wishes of its own citizens—and honour its own previous commitments—by accepting its legal borders. All Arab neighbours must pledge to honour Israel's right to live in peace under these conditions. The United States is squandering international prestige and goodwill and intensifying global anti-American terrorism by unofficially condoning or abetting the Israeli confiscation and colonization of Palestinian territories.

It will be a tragedy—for the Israelis, the Palestinians, and the world—if peace is rejected and a system of oppression, apartheid, and sustained violence is permitted to prevail.

These are tough words for Israeli politicians, though not necessarily for Israeli citizens, to hear, especially as they come not from someone who has always supported the Palestinians, not from someone expected to be anti-Israel and certainly not from an anti-Semite. No, the author is ex-President Jimmy Carter and this is an excerpt from his 2006 book, *Palestine: Peace Not Apartheid.*

I started out a great fan of Israel. In 1948, when Israel came into being, I was a high school student. The year before, a number of European Jewish kids had arrived after somehow avoiding the Holocaust. I saw the newscasts about the Holocaust. Most kids of my generation were taken to local theatres to see these horrors so we would understand what the war had been about. I saw the tattoos on the arms of surviving Jewish people. I followed the Nuremberg trials and was sickened by what I saw. So when the State of Israel was proclaimed, it seemed that this was indeed a nation for a people hitherto without a home, the home being their Biblical land. It made sense to me. Moreover, this land, so we were led to believe, was almost empty and weren't Jewish settlers renowned for turning deserts into flora a-blooming?

I didn't ask any questions then or even later as I went through university and into the workaday world. I did have a nagging concern, however, when I saw newsreels of Palestinian refugee camps containing I knew not how many people but obviously a lot. Where had they come from and why? What was to become of them?

In those days the story we were told went something like this: When Palestine was apportioned between Arab and Jew and after Israel was recognized by the US, the USSR and the United Nations, the new nation of Israel was attacked by Arab armies bent on destroying it. We were led to believe that Palestinians voluntarily gave up their homes and went elsewhere. One popular version was that they were urged by the Arab forces to leave their homes to make way for their invasion. The Israeli case was, for whatever reason, that these people had abandoned their homes, thereby entitling Israel to do with the land as it saw fit. The awkward bit was that while Jews from all over the world were entitled to "return" to Israel—even though they had never been there—it was not so for Palestinians who had, by fleeing, forfeited their right to return to their ancient homeland.

This issue is important because, while clearly Israel was a nation *de facto*, did that reality bestow a legal or moral right to expel those who had lived there for two thousand years and more? It was specifically *not* their right to do so according to UN resolution 194 (11), which "resolves that the refugees wishing to return to their homes and live at peace with their neighbours should be permitted to do so at the earliest practicable date, and that compensation should be paid for the property of those choosing not to return and for loss of or damage to property which, under principles of international law or in equity, should be made good by the governments or authorities responsible." While Israel calls itself a democracy based upon the rule of law, that case can only be made if it fairly treats non-Jews who remained *as well as* those who left. This would mean that Israeli

Arabs should have the same rights as Israeli Jews and that refugees should be entitled to return or to receive fair compensation.

Following the line of happenings from Israel's independence until now is a daunting task. There is no question that the Palestinians made a huge mistake in their early plane hijackings and brutal murders of people outside the struggle. They made even more of a mistake in targeting private citizens. But Israelis were scarcely innocent babes in the forest, making at least three fundamental errors in judgment.

1. They assumed a monopoly on virtue. History was rewritten to suit. The Arabs had no rights and their claim to return to lands stolen from them was illusory. Lands stolen by Israel are, it seems, deemed legitimate because God wants it that way.

2. Israel didn't match eye for an eye but took five eyes and then some. The casualties since the second *intifada* have been roughly five (some say four, as if that's important) Palestinians for one Israeli killed. It never occurs to Israeli governments that Israel is brutal and obsessed with taking revenge far in excess of what could be seen as reasonable. This, far from discouraging terrorism, has increased it. In following this policy the Israeli government seems unable to grasp that while they have modern weapons, including nuclear weapons in abundance, that Palestinians do not and rely entirely upon personal sacrifice, however odious that may be.

3. To plant Israeli settlements in occupied territory and continue that policy has made it plain that Israel has a brutal side and that their policies were wired to the need to keep right wing hawks onside lest the government fall.

In assessing a matter that is about 150 years old or more, it's unfortunately tempting to gloss over that with which you don't agree and match your facts to your prejudices. Just to look back to the end of World War I provides one with plenty of evidence to take either side unless, like President Carter, you are able to make dispassionate judgments. I think the underlying problem is that Israel, with highly subjective and self-serving piety, believes that it was entitled to have a state in Palestine, and that because the UN, US and Russia recognized their state in 1948, the Palestinians—never consulted even informally—have thus been fairly and justly treated. Since 1948 Israeli policy has been based upon not only their legal right but their moral and God-given right to what the UN decided was theirs— plus anything else they could lay their hands on. Thus the opposite is also true, namely, that the Palestinians have no legal rights, no moral rights and no spiritual rights to any of the land including the Occupied Territories and even beyond.

This is a comfortable view for Israelis to have, but would you as a Palestinian whose ancestors had occupied the lands for two thousand years, take such a charitable view? Suppose the Oregon Treaty of 1846 that put the boundary between BC and Washington at the 49th parallel were challenged by the US, and suppose the United Nations agreed that they should compromise their claim and only get the bottom half of BC. Would you in Vancouver accept that? Would you accept Americans coming in, knocking down your houses, dispossessing you and driving you north where refugee camps await? There is this difference, of course. Americans have never lived on our land— but come to think of it, neither had the Jews lived in Palestine for nearly two thousand years before Israel was formalized.

Canada's Middle East Policy

Thou art weighed in the balance and are found wanting.
*—*Daniel V. 27

L ooked at from a distance, Canada is a strange land. Large in size, small in population. Bilingual and multicultural. Old ties to Great Britain dwindling as it struggles with the giant next door. A country dealing with increasing regionalism as it gropes for a foreign policy.

The 1931 Statute of Westminster granted us independence and in September 1939 Canada symbolically declared war a week after Britain to demonstrate that independence. Yet when the UN was formed, the USSR was given seats for the Ukraine and Belarus to offset Britain's Commonwealth seats. Thus, as recently as 1945 after a brilliant war record as a nation, we were still seen as sort of an international stepchild, part of the family but different. One is reminded of former US Secretary of State Dean Acheson's cruel jibe that "Great Britain has lost an empire and has not yet found a role." Try as we have, Canadians still seek a role for their country with which they can be comfortable.

During the Cold War our policy was to snipe at America for hometown political brownie points while always remembering that we were on "their side" if trouble came. When the Cold War ended, Canada became less willing to accept the lead of the United States. Sadly, with the US now being the only superpower, it doesn't much matter to the White House what anyone else, let alone Canada, thinks. George W. Bush has made it clear that the US will do whatever it thinks best for its own interests, with those interests determined by the most recent polls. "You're either with us or against us," says this terrible president. Canadians don't like being in thrall to America yet are uncertain how to break free.

But now, like Bush, the Harper government uncritically supports Israeli policy. This is clearly wrong-headed. Canadians should stand back, survey the scene, learn the history and make a principled stand for a solution where both Palestinians and Israelis recognize realities, such as the fact that the Palestine/Israel populations are half and half Jews and Arabs while, within Israel itself, the Palestinian population is about 25 percent and growing. Israel, as the relative number of Jews in the region diminishes, sees itself besieged from without and faced with ever-increasingly hostile Palestinian Arabs within. Its consequent stubbornness brings more violence from surrounding Arab groups that seek Israel's destruction. Thus, stumbling blocks of land and the claims of Palestinian refugees seem unmovable. By firmly taking sides, the Harper government has disqualified itself as a possible arbitrator.

Israel has had, by far, the best of the PR war. Most Canadians believe, quite erroneously, that Palestinian Arabs willingly abandoned their homes in the 1948 War, so tough luck on them. Many look at the West Bank as "disputed lands" rather than "occupied lands," which they are. And most Canadians, evidently including Harper, believe that Israel's "land for peace" policy was fair, not understanding such a solution would leave Palestinians having to go through Israeli roadblocks to get from one part of their country to another. Quite apart from other considerations, Israeli blockades are well known to Palestinians for their long delays, constant hassling and physical brutality. And we shrug off the Jewish settlements in occupied lands, which are seen by Palestinians as an ongoing "up yours."

Canada must develop a policy of "honest broker," something it cannot do if it's on Israel's side whate'er betide. As Iran develops nuclear weapons and comes nose to nose with a nuclear-armed Israel, settling land and refugee claims becomes the only issue that matters. The refugee population has gone from about 700,000 in 1948 to well over 4,000,000 so obviously a settlement based on land alone won't happen. But put yourself in the position of one of these refugees: Any Jew from anywhere in the world has a "right to return" to Israel, a country he's never seen, while Palestinians are denied the right to return home to what was theirs for over two thousand years.

The stakes are mortal. Canada, if it is to help, must unshackle itself from its present policy of blindly supporting Israel and seek policies aimed at achieving justice for Palestinians *and* Israelis. Otherwise the price to be paid could well be Armageddon.

Two Jews Look at Israel

Two very important books, each written by an Israeli Jew, attempt to shatter Israel's claim of "inheriting" land abandoned by Palestinians and make the case for Israeli Arabs enjoying the same rights and privileges as Israeli Jews. Susan Nathan emigrated to Israel when she was in her fifties, automatically becoming an Israeli citizen. She moved to Tamra, a town of about 25,000 and was the only Jew in the place. Her book, *The Other Side of Israel*, tells a shocking story of how Israeli-Palestinians are treated. Their towns and villages receive much less financial assistance than do Israeli ones; ditto their schools, healthcare needs and their right to move freely in the country. Their land is regularly expropriated by force and without compensation, and they are constantly harassed—too often brutalized, indeed killed—by Israeli soldiers if they travel, even if it's to go to work.

But it's the second book that sent shivers down my spine. Ilan Pappé is an Israeli academic with a BA from Hebrew University and a PhD from Oxford. He's a senior lecturer in political science at Haifa University and is the academic director of the Research Institute for Peace at Givat Haviva. His latest book, *The Ethnic Cleansing of Palestine,* is a shocker. The dust jacket relates:

> The 1948 Palestine-Israel War is known to Israelis as "The War of Independence," but for Palestinians it will forever be the Nakba, the "catastrophe." Before, during and after this war—as the state of Israel came into being—occurred one of the largest forced migrations in modern history. Around a million Palestinians were expelled from their homes at gunpoint, thousands of civilians were massacred, and hundreds of Palestinian villages were deliberately destroyed. Though the truth about the mass expulsion has been systematically distorted and suppressed, had it taken place in the twenty-first century it could only have been called "ethnic cleansing."

Having read the book, I can assure you that this dust jacket accurately sums up Dr. Pappé's case. Whether it's a fair or accurate case I can not say. His fundamental position is that the emptying of hundreds of Palestinian towns and villages was anything but voluntary; that prior to, during and after the 1948 war, Israelis systematically drove residents from their homes and that thousands including children were massacred. One of the more famous of these "ethnic cleansings," as Dr. Pappé describes them, was at Dawaymeh on October 28, 1948, where Israeli troops (Battalion 89 of Brigade 8) killed some four hundred villagers, including women and children while expelling about six thousand others. In answer to the Israeli position of a voluntary exodus, Dr. Pappé says, on page 131 that "it should be clear by now that the Israeli foundational myth about a voluntary Palestinian flight the war started—in response to a call by Arab leaders to make way for invading armies—holds no water. It is a sheer fabrication that there were Jewish attempts, as Israeli textbooks still insist today, to persuade Palestinians to stay. As we have seen, hundreds of thousands of

Palestinians had already been expelled by force *before the war began*, [emphasis added] and tens of thousands more would be expelled in the first week of the war ..." The book goes on to tell of rape and death as Israelis "cleansed" 531 villages as it expelled more than half the Arab population.

Ilan Pappé has his detractors, and I would suggest that readers "google" him and read what the opposition has to say. My own conclusion is that he's of the "academic left," much in the image of Noam Chomsky. Probably Pappé's sharpest critics—at least among those that I could find—are Janet Levy and Dr. Roberta Seid, who say this, in part:

> "The most hated Israeli in Israel"—an ignoble moniker to be sure—has not eroded Ilan Pappé's star power on US college campuses, where he is more often than not warmly greeted. The usual contingent of [Edward] Said acolytes, Chomsky groupies and a panoply of pro-Palestinian student organizations are invariably well-represented in his audiences. The prominence of resolutely anti-Israel partisans is unsurprising, given Pappé's role as one of Israel's most prominent die-hard Marxists. Pappé was invited to UCLA by history professor and fellow Edward Said disciple, Gabriel Piterberg. A call to the university revealed that history department professors may invite speakers at their own discretion using departmental funding to cover expenses for colloquia without any oversight. This practice enables faculty to freely promulgate their political agendas and control the degree to which students are presented with alternative views and critiques. Piterberg has been labeled "an avant-garde radical who harangues campus demonstrations, endorses petitions and teaches a course in post-and anti-Zionism."

But the point is not what we think of Dr. Pappé or Ms. Nathan as people but whether or not their evidence is sufficiently accurate to cast serious doubt upon the "official" history put out by the State of Israel. The reason this is in issue is not just that people like you and me need to know the truth but because, if Pappé's and Nathan's arguments have substance, there'll be no peace in the Middle East until the wrongs are settled. For Israel the time is short. Palestinians who demand the right to return are increasing rapidly. And the number of Palestinian Arabs already in Israel will continue to increase and will one day have enough members in the Knesset to negate the Jews ability to govern. And absent a settlement, Israel, a nuclear power, will be missile-to-missile with Iran, who'll soon be in the nuclear club.

Dr. Pappé's and Ms Nathan's books cannot be trashed by ad hominem attacks. They are either right or wrong. But if the issues they raise are not satisfactorily dealt with, the believers in the Armageddon of the *Book of Revelation* may be right after all.

Whither the Left?

W hen the Soviet Union imploded not long after its Eastern
European satellites found freedom, there was a great sigh
of relief in the West, accompanied, sadly, by chest-thumping trium-
phalism. We had won and we had proved that capitalism is better
than communism. Of course, it did that all right, but what it didn't
prove was that raw, laissez-faire capitalism was better than any other
system. The West, led by the United States, then ignored Russia and
her plight: There having been no effective opposition to communist
rule for seventy-five years, there was no government-in-waiting when
the USSR collapsed. It was close to anarchy as the hero president,
Boris Yeltsin—whether because of booze or illness—could not deal
effectively with the gangsterism that accompanied the sell-off of
public assets. Where a short time earlier the rich people had been
the party bosses, now as new "entrepreneurs," they became instant
billionaires.

Not only was the US not of much help, under its pressure a number of the former satellites of the Soviet Union not only asked and
got membership in the European Community, they joined NATO as

well. What better way to "stick it" to the Russians than have former Warsaw Pact countries join Russia's old enemy, NATO? One must also ask of what value were these countries to NATO unless it was to increase the threat to Moscow. It was a dumb move, and it lit a slow burning fuse that burns ever faster each day.

It can and has been argued that the breakup of the Soviet Union impeded the march, albeit a slow one, to democracy which Gorbachev's reforms had started. In any event, by 1992 communism in the world was finished except in Cuba and North Korea, unless one considers China a communist nation, which most don't.

You might think that the collapse of the Soviet Union would have ended the activities of leftist groups, whereas, in fact, it has enhanced them and for several reasons. Moscow had been a high maintenance friend to leftists. Not only did they have to spread their own dogma but they had to constantly explain that they weren't communists and they didn't take orders from the USSR even though they were saying the same things. This became a problem when patriotism was called for, such as in the Cold War, the Korean War, the Vietnam War and Russia going into Afghanistan. What also happened was that capitalism provided a whole new playing field for the left.

First, the left was able to claim, with much truth, that the capitalist world contained some pretty nasty governments that were no better at the democracy bit than Russia was. The poor, despite what economists like Milton Friedman preached, were getting poorer and saw no hope. Canadians and Americans went through an interesting metamorphosis: While unemployment was often low, neither country counted the people who had been forced to take lower-paying jobs because their companies had shut down and outsourced to China. But it was not only the labour force that was hit; so was middle management. Youngish executives, having at last reached the point where they could afford a golf club and skating lessons for their kids, had to take lower wages in less challenging jobs. In short, globalism, through world free trade, has created a whole new clientele for the left, whose leader is probably a Canadian woman, Naomi Klein. In her latest book *The Shock Doctrine: The Rise of Disaster Capitalism*, Ms. Klein documents—and that's the right word—the sordid record left by many capitalist countries, especially Chile, Argentina and Brazil, and she uses these examples to lay the basis for her argument that pure capitalism, as Milton Friedman and his acolytes would have it, is evil.

It's not my task here to debate Ms. Klein's propositions but to point out that the left, far from having abandoned the battlefield, is very much on it and spoiling for a jousting. The left is fractured, of course. Within its ranks are the hard-core conservatives who keep the flickering candle of communism alive if not well. Then there is the Green Party whose members are largely on the left but unable to see much use in traditional left wing parties because they are no more environmentalists than capitalists are when jobs—real or, as in the case of local fish farms, fictional—are at stake. And there is another dynamic as well. In order to gain power, the traditional left has moved much towards the centre, thus marginalizing much of their old political base. The new left isn't pure dogma anymore. They've learned from recent history that there is room for good social policy, good environmental policy and decent profits.

To See Ourselves as Putin Sees Us

Is Vladimir Putin a democrat at heart who, even though he spent most of his life as a communist in the KGB, wants Russia to be an open and democratic state?

I don't often review books in my own books, but I beg leave to make an exception. *Kremlin Rising: Vladimir Putin's Russia and the End of Revolution* is written by a husband and wife team, Peter Baker and Susan Glasser, who spent nearly five years in the Moscow bureau of the *Washington Post*. Their book deals with the unbelievable rise of Vladimir Putin, through the inexplicable support of Boris Yeltsin, to the presidency of Russia. It takes the reader through the horrific slaughter of the Breslan schoolchildren and the unbelievably bungled rescue of those held hostage by Chechen rebels in a Moscow theatre. That chapter alone will keep your eyes glued. Baker and Glasser write about the instant billionaires and how one was smart enough to take Putin's hint to go elsewhere—he bought the Chelsea Football Club—while the richest of them all, Mikhail Khodorkovsky, stubbornly laughed off Putin's not-so-subtle suggestion that he return some of his loot and now languishes in a

Moscow jail. And we see how Putin, once a KGB officer, has put so many of its members in power that they are the core of his ever-increasing authority.

The book's overall message is clear: Putin is now a virtual dictator running what he calls a "managed democracy" and the people of Russia approve by a wide margin. In its long history, Russia has always had an autocrat in charge, and the Russian people, while scarcely yearning for the return of the old Soviet Union, badly want law and order and a better style of living. Putin is bringing both so the average Muscovite asks, "What do I care that Putin controls the media and has taken most of the power away from the Duma? Bad people are going to jail and my lot is getting better."

But the book's message is one that George W. Bush simply doesn't understand. Western democracy, so-called, is not for everyone. In fact, Russians look at the UK and the US and see managed democracies whose leaders seem to be simply elected dictatorships, just as in Russia. And as Russians look at the Patriot Bill and other anti-terrorist initiatives passed by the Bush Administration, they might well see themselves as having the freer country. There is no question that Putin has strangled dissent. All the TV stations that count now take their marching orders from the Kremlin as do most of the newspapers. And Putin uses the resources of the state to get public support. The Russians were humiliated by the break-up of the Soviet Union and any leader in the Kremlin knows that this must be dealt with. Russians see that their nation's old allies have become members of NATO, and now that the Bush government is to go ahead with a missile shield in Europe, pretending that only "rogue states" are the driving force, Putin will modernize his weaponry and aim it again at European cities. The question then arises as to whether or not Putin will step down in 2008 or have the constitution amended so that he can seek another term. At this writing he has his eye on becoming prime minister and moving the seat of power to his office from that of the president. The worry, of course, is that while Putin remains a reasonably benign dictator, the history of dictators tells us that once all power is gained, the benignity evaporates.

This book should be read by all who feel the need to understand what Russia will be doing in the years to come.

Human Rights, Bush-Style

America is the land of liberty, right? The country that lives under the rule of law, okay? I'm sure, therefore, that all lovers of liberty will be heartened by President Bush's announcement that alleged terrorist prisoners held by the United States will not be subject to all sorts of torture, only approved kinds, and that they will be eligible for trial by a military (US) court. What is this sudden blasé public attitude towards torture? How can there be an "acceptable" form of torture? And what is acceptable torture—just any torture that doesn't show on the body? Even if you can swallow this horrible breach of human rights, how reliable are confessions under torture, anyway?

It's unclear from Dubya's statement whether or not the tortures at Abu Ghraib and Guantanamo Bay are within the allowable torture now set out by his administration. Presumably they are since much of the brutality in those places was mental not physical. It's a tricky bit of new lawmaking. Stung by the Supreme Court decision granting rights to US prisoners, the proposed legislation takes pains to ensure that the Supreme Court will not have a second bite at the apple. As one law professor says, "The act makes clear . . . that the Geneva

Conventions are not a source of judicially enforceable individual rights." Other legal experts say it adds up to an apparently unique interpretation of the Geneva Conventions, one that could allow CIA operatives and others to use many of the very techniques disavowed by the Pentagon, including stress positions, sleep deprivation and extreme temperatures. All this is necessary, says President Bush, in order to save American lives. That, of course, is the rationale of all who would take away liberty. Hitler and the Gestapo used torture to, in their minds, save Nazi lives.

The example that's always trotted out is what if there was a huge terrorist attack, another 9/11 planned? Would the authorities be permitted to torture someone thought to know the plans? This is the standard technique of using the worst-case scenario in order to justify a lesser evil. This is how you justify torture at all levels. Take the worst scenario and extend it to anyone you suspect of anything. So are we to accept the word of George Bush, Richard Cheney and former Defense Secretary Donald Rumsfeld that these prisoners are to be deprived of trial in a civil court with lawyers because to give them justice would be to encourage terrorism? Is their confidence in the American justice system so low that they don't think the United States of America will be treated fairly by the regular American judiciary?

But here is the fatal flaw: While the United States is preaching the rule of law and democracy to countries in the Middle East and says it wants these things for Iraq, it denies democracy and the rule of law to its own prisoners when it no longer suits American presidents and their lackeys. Saddam Hussein gets a trial with whatever legal help he needs while "lesser" prisoners are held, often incommunicado, *tortured* for over five years and must rot in jail. That's the American way? Surely to God the United States must allow lesser prisoners the same sort of open trial Saddam Hussein got!

If you were an Iraqi or any other citizen living under a dictatorship, how much appeal would democracy, George Bush-style, have for you?

The Worst of Them All

Probably the worst president in American history is George W. Bush. I say this because the worst of them all hitherto—Warren Harding, Andrew Johnson and Ulysses S. Grant—did not imperil the safety of their country—and indeed the world. Bush Junior has not only put the United States at a huge risk, which now threatens to become a certainty, but he's put the entire world on the edge of a deep fiery hole.

It's now certain that Bush went into Iraq on a false premise, the only question being, did he know that or was he merely stupid? But no, it's worse that that. He, former Defense Secretary Donald Rumsfeld, Vice-President Richard Cheney and, sad to say, Colin Powell all lied to the American public, the United Nations and the world community. Then having gone into Iraq, the United States had far too few troops on the ground, a situation that it now seems clear was caused by the Bush administration, namely then-Defense Secretary Donald Rumsfeld, overruling the military. So not only did Bush make a catastrophic political error, he and his "team," without a particle of military training, overruled the experts. These errors have killed close to four thusand American service personnel and tens of thousands of Iraqis. (He'd better have an "in" with God when his Judgment Day arrives.)

It mustn't be supposed that Bush simply made an error in his judgment of the evidence before him. One of the reasons given for the invasion—a reason that became more and more popular with his administration as the evidence demonstrated that Saddam Hussein had no WMDs—was that Saddam Hussein and Al Qaeda were partners in 9/11. Even though Cheney has been caught out on this lie, he and the Republican administration continue to peddle it.

And remember how Dubya was going to take Osama bin Laden "dead or alive"? This was the purpose of the US invasion of Afghanistan. But the US, instead of pursuing bin Laden, pulled their punches so they could invade Iraq. What we now have is a Taliban and an Al Qaeda very much on the upsurge, leaving no doubt that, tragically, they'll be heard from again.

What Bush has accomplished is to get the entire Muslim world pissed off at the West even though some of their governments are officially friendly. However, those "friendly countries" such as Egypt, Saudi Arabia and Jordan are just waiting for an Islamic coup. Pakistan is also a just coup away from an Islamic dictatorship. All the while Iran, which is a theocracy, is getting nuclear arms ready to aim at Tel Aviv and other Israeli cities, while what appeared to be a great American success story, Afghanistan—now with all but a couple of cities back in the hands of the Taliban—is demonstrating why even Alexander the Great couldn't conquer it. It will remain a festering boil. Bush, having ploughed into this ungodly mess is now, like Bre'r Rabbit, stuck to the Tar Baby. Those old enough to have watched the events in Vietnam will, no doubt, have that eerie feeling of "Here we go again!"

Despite the fact that in March 2003 Bush declared victory in Iraq, the situation there has deteriorated into a civil war that no amount of American and British soldiers can stop from going on ad infinitum. It's obvious that Bush envisioned pretty girls flinging flowers and other things at the heroic invading soldiers. He knew nothing about the racial and religious divides within the country and is now without any support by Muslims the world over and is forced to rely upon unpopular dictators to cheer him up.

You may recall that after his first election the new president of the United States couldn't tell a reporter the name of the president of Pakistan. (And yes, maybe you couldn't either but you're not the president of the United States!) The India/Pakistan/Bangladesh/ Sri Lanka area is several seething cauldrons of political unrest with two of the countries, India and Pakistan, possessing nuclear weapons while they each covet Kashmir (over which they have already fought two wars). But while not knowing that General Pervez Musharraf was the dictator of Pakistan may be forgivable (though I don't know how), Bush didn't even know about the three different groups of people within Iraq and that the Sunnis, the minority Arab group, ran the country under Saddam Hussein, that the nation's Shias, the majority, were backed by Iran, and that the Kurds had virtually a state unto themselves and that they had real issues with the rest of the country over oil, especially in the Kirkuk region. He also didn't seem to know that, before he shot off his mouth about an "evil axis," relations between Iran and America had been getting better and better. He obviously didn't know that in political terms "axis" means an alliance and North Korea, Iran and Saddam Hussein's Iraq was scarcely that. And Mr. Bush and his party, thick as planks the lot of them, didn't think they needed friends for their meddling plans but they did, and apart from Britain and Australia, they had none. Now both of these "friends" look to be parting company with him. Leaving aside that Hitler didn't give the *Wehrmacht* winter clothing when they invaded Russia, this military exercise by Mr. Bush has to be the most colossal blunder of all time.

This clown makes Andrew Johnson, Millard Fillmore and Warren Harding look like geniuses. But when these guys were in power, they didn't have the ability to blow the world to smithereens in a nanosecond. This in itself puts George W. Bush in a class by himself and wearing the dunce's cap.

PART III

Canadian Concerns

Mr. Moneybags Is Here—Again

I t's November 19, 2007, and I have just arrived home from a wonderful three-week cruise. I open the *National Post* and there it is: The Mulroney/Schreiber/Airbus/bags-of-money story is in the headlines yet again! And this time Prime Minister Harper has ordered a probe—after refusing on November 2 to reopen the Airbus file by arguing that "This is not a route that I want to go down, and I don't think that, if the Liberal Party thought twice about it, it is a power they would want to give me" because, he says coyly, he would then be tempted to take another look at controversies that plagued former Liberal prime ministers. Has Canadian politics really descended to governing by blackmail?

The answer is, sadly, yes. To give a brief example, hearken back to the 1980s when the Liberals formed an illegal cartel to boost the price of uranium after the US cancelled its contract to buy from us. There was all hell to pay from the opposition Tories who demanded a probe, and Prime Minister Trudeau finally appointed a senior civil servant, Robert Bertrand, to do it. In due course, his findings were delivered to the government, which promptly buried his report.

During the election of 1984 I was assured by several Tory candidates that, if they formed the government, the Bertrand Report would be made public. Mr. Mulroney's Tories won and the report remained unreleased. One cannot, then, ignore the strong inference that Prime Minister Mulroney, in keeping a lid on the matter, was giving a message to the Liberals that said, "We won't look for crawlies under Liberal rocks so long as you extend us the same courtesy."

So when I concluded my research on this latest development regarding Mr. Mulroney and Mr. Schreiber, I asked myself why Prime Minister Harper suddenly took an interest in the matter. To me the answer was that Mr. Harper saw this becoming an airing of Tory Party shenanigans going back to 1983 when Karlheinz Schreiber had supported Brian Mulroney's political assassination of Joe Clark. Clearly, Schreiber badly wants to sing. He feels betrayed by Mulroney who did nothing to prevent his extradition to Germany. Mr. Harper, in a no-win situation, felt that it was better that the Tories order a "probe" and thus seem to be in favour of openness rather than let it become a cause celebre over which they had no control. If he hadn't done this, people would tar the present Tories with the sins of the past. This way he can say, "Look, that's ancient history as far as we're concerned." In short, Mr. Harper had two options, one that was terrible and another that was only bad.

Now according to my dictionary, the word "probe" means "a penetrating or critical investigation." Is this what Prime Minister Harper intends as he orders a "probe" into the business affairs of Brian Mulroney? Or will it be confined to a bit of a look-see into the $300,000 in cash the former PM received from the Airbus Mr. Fix-it, Karlheinz Schreiber? If the latter, neither the Canadian public nor, Mr. Mulroney, if he's innocent, will be well served.

The issue is a serious one indeed. In 1988, while Mr. Mulroney was prime minister, Airbus sold thirty-four A-320 jets for $1.8 billion to Air Canada, which was then a federal Crown corporation. Karlheinz Schreiber was the de facto owner of a Liechtenstein company called

IAL that brokered the deal. Contrary to what Mr. Mulroney said under oath in 1998 (more later), in fact, he knew Schreiber well, had received financial help from him in his 1983 campaign to unseat PC leader Joe Clark and, in fact, had pressured Schreiber, upon completion of the Airbus deal, to pay a fat commission to Mulroney's crony the late Frank Moores. Mr. Mulroney doesn't deny receiving this money from Mr. Schreiber, a fugitive from German justice whose innocence is, to put it mildly, compromised by the hugely expensive fight he has conducted to avoid extradition.

But these questions about that $300,000 in cash payments arise:

- Were these payments negotiated with Mr. Mulroney while he was still in office? Karlheinz Schreiber says they were.
- Given the continually changing versions, what, in fact, was this money for?
- Was this a legal retainer? If so, do Mr. Mulroney and the huge law firm in which he's a partner customarily take their retainers in payments of large amounts of cash in shopping bags?
- If these payments were eventually made to Mr. Mulroney's law firm, Ogilvy Renault, was a receipt given by the firm? And what did they do with all this cash, bearing in mind that Canadian banks will only take deposits up to $10,000 in cash?
- If the payments were to Mulroney, and they were for legal fees, surely he had to report this to his law firm or be guilty of breach of trust because members of a legal partnership generally can't do legal work on the side. This raises another question: Has anyone demanded an accounting by Ogilvy Renault as to whether they got the money and, if they did, how they dealt with the cash?

All these questions must be taken in the context of a *National Post* article published on November 9, 2007, which said in part, "Businessman Karlheinz Schreiber alleges in an affidavit filed in court yesterday that an advisor to former prime minister Brian

Mulroney requested a transfer of funds to Mr. Mulroney's lawyer in Geneva related to the Airbus deal."

• Mr. Mulroney claims he paid income tax on this money but says the details are "nobody's goddamn business." But in order to clear his name, shouldn't he make his tax returns public at least insofar as they deal with these cash exchanges?

• If this money was paid to Mr. Mulroney directly for his prospective legal fees, did he deposit the funds into a trust account as the law requires of all lawyers?

• On this matter, the CBC reports the following: "Former Prime Minister Brian Mulroney, who received $300,000 in cash from German-Canadian deal maker Karlheinz Schreiber in 1993 and 1994, did not pay taxes on the payments in the years he received the money." The CBC then points out that "the former prime minister filed a voluntary tax disclosure some time later. The *Globe and Mail* and CBC's *Fifth Estate* have learned that he took advantage of an option that the Canada Revenue Agency offers for people who have previously filed inaccurate returns and subsequently decide to correct the record." Why, I ask, didn't Mulroney file his tax returns honestly when they were due? Are we to understand that when the taxes were due, these payments slipped his mind?

But the matter scarcely ends there.

• There is the overriding question, where did Schreiber *get* $300,000 in cash, a daunting task indeed?

• Given the fact that Mulroney sued the federal government— because the RCMP, in order to get information from Swiss banks, had to state that they had grounds to do so—and got $2.1 million for his pains, why didn't Mulroney also sue the CBC's *Fifth Estate* broadcast on February 8, 2006, for the comments they aired that, if not true, were clearly libellous?

• According to an interview given by Schreiber to *Fifth Estate*, Brian Mulroney visited Zurich on February 2, 1998, to "reassure himself" that there would not be any evidence that he had received any money from a certain bank. This statement raises this obvious question: In light of the fact that this was *after* he'd received $300,000 from Schreiber, was Mulroney trying to make sure that these payments would be kept confidential? If so, why? Considering Mulroney's present story that the money came from Schreiber as a legal retainer, why would he feel it necessary to do this?

Throughout this saga, a Swiss bank account named BRITAN has kept popping up and Schreiber claims it was from this account he paid Mulroney, which prompts these questions:

• Is BRITAN a codeword for BRIAN?

• Did—indeed, *does*—Mulroney have any money in any bank account in Switzerland, and if so, did it come from Karlheinz Schreiber? Did, does it, bear any relationship to the Airbus deal?

• What was the true relationship between Mulroney and Schreiber? Back in 1996, when being questioned under oath on his libel case against the RCMP, Mulroney denied a friendship with Schreiber, claiming that the man was just an acquaintance with whom he had a couple of cups of coffee. In light of the fact that this evidence came long after Mulroney received the $300,000 from Schreiber, was Mulroney's testimony not perjury? If he had answered honestly, would that not have automatically prompted the question: "Have you had any business dealings with Schreiber?" Would not Mulroney then have been faced with either disclosing the details of the $300,000 deal or committing perjury? Does this amount to untrue testimony that took the RCMP away from their investigations while at the same time suppressing the $300,000 matter? Former Justice Minister Allan Rock says, that had the government known of the true relationship between Mulroney and Schreiber, it would never have bought off Mulroney's lawsuit for $2.1 million. This prompts the obvious question: shouldn't we get our money back?

- If these are valid questions, what has the Solicitor General's office done about it?

I've commented extensively elsewhere (See, for example, thetyee.ca for January 29, 2007) on the reluctance of Canada's "old boy" media to investigate this entire matter, but I have not raised this matter of great importance to Canadians: The RCMP has throughout this affair behaved as if they act or don't act depending on how tight their political masters hold their leash. Is this because the commissioner of the RCMP, long independent of government, is now a deputy minister to the Solicitor General and thus subject to political direction? Which leads to one more question:

- Were the activities of the RCMP in this entire matter directed, in whole or in part, by their political masters?

This is not a matter of a political vendetta against former Prime Minister Mulroney but rather an attempt to raise issues which must be dealt with. The facts as we know them and the questions they have prompted raise serious questions about Mr. Mulroney's actions while in office. If they are not satisfactorily answered, many Canadians will believe that Brian Mulroney, in Stevie Cameron's famous phrase, was "on the take." If Mr. Mulroney is innocent of any wrongdoing, it's in his interest to have this entire affair thoroughly examined. But whether he's innocent or not, Canadians have the right to know what the real story is.

Authors run the constant risk that time will make redundant a position they have taken. I run that risk here, but no matter what happens in the Mulroney case, I humbly submit that the results of my research into the matter stand alone as fair questions that the reader will be able to use when assessing the life and political morals of Brian Mulroney.

The Power of the MP

I've written much on the subject of the power—or lack of it—of members of parliament before and wouldn't deal with it again had the Liberals and Conservatives not promised to deal with the "democracy deficit" in the 2006 election. In fact, at this writing both the prime minister and the leader of the opposition have disciplined members for speaking their minds.

I'm astonished at the public ignorance of how our system works, though "doesn't work" may be a better way of saying it. Not long ago when I was chairing a meeting for the Greater Vancouver Regional District, a lady, well spoken and obviously very bright, told us all that if the government didn't do what they were supposed to do, why, it was up to us voters to get a better legislature or House of Commons because this was, after all, a democracy. This breathtaking naïveté prevails throughout Canada. Is this because all parties have an unsaid agreement that the parliamentary farce will continue?

Democracy, the rights and privileges of MPs and MLAs, died long ago. The right of the people, through the ballot box, to expect that members of parliament will look after the people's affairs is an illusion.

Prime Minister Harper's expulsion of John Cummins, Conservative MP from Delta-Richmond East, from the Fisheries Committee makes it breathtaking clear that Mr. Cummins was not elected to represent his constituency or his conscience but to do what he's told.

Cummins is a maverick in that he truly believes in representative democracy. His riding, a coastal one that depends in large measure on the health of the British Columbia salmon fishery, has since 1993 elected Mr. Cummins, a former commercial fisherman, to protect their interests, a mandate he takes very seriously. In 2006 the multi-flawed Fisheries Act came before the Commons Fisheries Committee upon which Mr. Cummins sat. Now the Department of Fisheries and Oceans has been a disaster on the West Coast since the Mulroney days when it was politicized in order to accommodate Alcan's Kemano Completion Project, which would have been an environmental catastrophe. And if the governments of the day hadn't buried a full DFO study of the Alcan plan, the project never would have got as far as it did. This study was done by the solid, soon-to-be ex-DFO scientists, who strongly condemned the project on environmental grounds. The report stayed suppressed until a copy was leaked to me in 1994 during the heated public debate that saw the project tubed by the Harcourt government. This same department, instead of acting as the policeman in the environment, has become a shill for the fish farming industry that is wiping out wild BC salmon. And no one has followed these and other West Coast fisheries debacles more thoroughly than Mr. Cummins.

Yet when Mr. Cummins, an expert on the West Coast fishery, made his opinions of the new Fisheries Act known to the Fisheries Committee, the Prime Minister yanked him! What the hell kind of parliamentary democracy is this? The issue here is not just Mr. Cummins' opinions but whether as an MP he can not only express them but try to have them implemented.

Both Prime Minister Harper and Mr. Cummins come from the Reform Party, where one of its raisons d'être was to bring in parliamentary reform, very much including allowing MPs themselves to make the appointments to various Commons committees, to appoint the chairs and to debate matters without the government whip telling them what to discuss or how to vote.

During the run-up to the 2006 election we heard the term "democracy deficit" for the first time and, by golly, Mr. Harper would see the independence of Commons committees as paramount to Commons reforms. But here are the comments on Cummins dismissal from the Conservative whip, Jay Hill: "We have to have all of our committee members solidly onside with the government's agenda. . . . You can imagine how it would look . . . if, at committee, we were to lose the entire bill because of one vote, and it was Mr. Cummins' vote." In other words, we'd rather have a bad bill pass than let one of our backbenchers "show up" the ministry's inadequacies. The Fisheries minister, says Mr. Hill, must not look bad just because someone who knows something about the subject expresses an adverse criticism.

The proof of my position has come about because we have a minority Tory government. When there is a majority, parliamentary committees are as valuable as tits on a bull. They are all, with the exception of the Public Accounts Committee, run by government MPs on orders from the prime minister through the party whip. The agenda is set by the government MP sitting as chair who can call or not call meetings, direct the agenda and control what government members say. The majority of the committee members are, of course, government MPs selected by the Prime Minister.

In November 2007 the House Committee on Ethics, by a six-to-five vote, decided to hold hearings into the dealings of former Tory prime minister Brian Mulroney and the infamous Karlheinz Schreiber. The five against were the Tory members. In short, if Mr. Harper had a majority, this matter would never have been on the agenda much less voted upon. With a minority one can see the light of day on issues a majority government would stonewall.

We are taught in school that we have "responsible government," which means that the prime minister and cabinet are hostage to the approval of the House of Commons. The reality is quite the opposite. In fact, the prime minister controls the House of Commons in many ways, not the least of which is his power to refuse to sign a naughty MP's nomination papers. Many people, dare I say most people, don't understand that for a person to run in a federal election under a party banner that party's leader must sign the nomination form. This is the power of political capital punishment. It is a huge weapon that MPs don't need reminding of. If they do, they need only look to the classic example John Nunziata who, like all Liberal candidates in 1993, promised to repeal the Goods and Services Tax. When, after the Liberal victory the minister of finance brought in a budget that didn't get rid of the GST, Nunziata voted against it. He had, after all, promised his constituents that it being Liberal Party policy, he would do so. Nunziata was tossed out of the Liberal caucus and Prime Minister Chrétien refused to sign his nomination papers in 1997.

Pause and think about this for a moment. Every MP knows that, if in representing his constituency and province he in any way offends the prime minister, that prime minister can, in effect, keep him from winning his seat again. That is one hell of a sword of Damocles that effectively eliminates the word "democracy" from the term "parliamentary democracy." Nunziata and Cummins demonstrate that Canadian MPs have about as much power as did a member of the old Soviet Presidium. Pierre Trudeau once said that, fify yards off the Hill, MPs were nobodies. I have always wondered why the geographical limitation. MPs are nobodies, period. Parliament is run by the prime minister's office by the prime minister on the advice on unelected advisors. Not since the fall of Sir John A. Macdonald over the 1873 Pacific Scandal has a majority government fallen and in Macdonald's day there was nothing like the party discipline we see today.

The good electors of Delta-Richmond East have been informed that democracy, Harper-style, hasn't changed, which is to say there is none. As with the bad old Libs, MPs are not allowed to represent their constituents nor permitted to fulfill election promises but are ciphers to do and say precisely as they are told, the penalty for disobeying being a political death sentence. John Cummins is a good man, an honourable man, a man who listens to his constituents and who tries to represent them—a fatal combination for a member of the Canadian House of Commons.

Budget Secrecy and All That Nonsense

I don't take government budgets very seriously. In fact, the budget process underscores the unassailable argument that the legislature is as democratic as was the pre-1989 Polish Parliament. The pre-budget "lockup" of the media and other favoured folk is plain humbug because, to start with, anyone who reads the papers or watches the news knows what's going to be in the budget. Moreover, no matter what it says, it will pass because not one single MLA from the government side dare question it, let alone vote against a single line of it, and the opposition will vote against all of it because that's what oppositions do.

The parliamentary rule is that if a finance minister leaks any part of the budget, however insignificant the leak may be, he/she must resign. More humbug. The classic case was that of Hugh Dalton who in 1947, as chancellor of the exchequer in the Attlee Labour government, just prior to delivering the budget, told a reporter—are you ready for this?—that there would be a tax of one penny on a pint of beer and a tax on dog racing. No one for a second thought that the pubs would fill up with those trying to beat the tax—they were already full to brimming anyway—and there was no indication of dog owners abandoning their pooches and taking up honest work. But not only did Dalton have to resign, he had these words of the prime minister echoing in his ears: "He's a perfect ass," said Mr. Attlee and added, "The principle of the inviolability of the budget is of the highest importance, and the discretion of the chancellor of the exchequer must be beyond question."

In 1989, federal finance minister Marc Lalonde had his budget speech leaked to a reporter and he simply added $200 million to the numbers, gave a Gallic shrug and went on about his business. So, since no one worries about leaks anymore, why do they have a lockup? The answer should not surprise you. The lockup, new shoes for the minister, powerful guests in the chamber and all that folderol are shams needed because the entire system is a sham, a fact which governments somehow manage to keep from the people. It's all humbug, play acting. It doesn't matter what the budget is, the government will secure its approval right after the tribal custom of a couple of speeches and an immaterial debate on "estimates." I've been there and almost the entire legislative process is humbug. The only positive thing to come out of the place is the occasional good question fired at the government by an opposition member. Apart from that, the legislature is a rubber stamp for the premier and his cabinet, and I need not remind you who hires and fires cabinet ministers.

Instead of treating the budgeting process as democracy in action, it's time we all had the wit to understand that the only democracy in our system is that every four years we get to elect who will be unrestrained dictator for the next four. The brutal truth is that we continue to act like the ten-year-old who, against all the evidence, still believes in Santa Claus.

Who Will Watch the Watchman?

"It is not merely of some importance but is of fundamental importance that justice should not only be done, but should manifestly and undoubtedly be seen to be done," wrote Lord Hewart in the case of *Rex v. Sussex Justices; Ex parte McCarthy*. What the learned judge was saying was that, while it's commendable to come to the right conclusion, you must do so in such a way that it at least looked as if you did it the right way; that appearances are important and perhaps even more important than the decision itself.

And so we come to the appointment of judges, which has always been a tricky business. Someone has to appoint them, so the "trick" for governments has always been to appoint someone who looks okay while ensuring he/she is a "safe pair of hands" for the government in power. Leaving aside the Provincial Court of BC, which I'll return to, the federal government has always relied upon two resources: First, the public has a high regard for judges and assumes that those appointed will be fair and, second and most important, most of the time the general public has never heard of the guy/gal before.

It's not just that prime ministers, who in effect appoint whomever they wish, have always just rewarded the party faithful, but that sometimes, as in the case of my highly estimable classmate Tom Berger, an exception will be made. And sometimes the reason for appointment to the Supreme Court of Canada will have a political significance larger than just making room for a pal at the public trough. However, apart from a few exceptions, it does appear that lawyers from the governing party have a distinct edge.

First a bit of background. Amongst its powers, the Supreme Court of Canada decides constitutional issues that arise between the federal government and provinces, yet the judges are all appointed by the head of the federal government! Talk about a conflict of interest! The argument has always been "these men and women, being elevated to the big bench, are free from politics and thus thoroughly independent." Really? Hearken back to the quote from Lord Hewart, above. Suppose you have a dispute with your neighbour and the judge is his brother. Would you accept the fact that he is fair-minded and that his adoption of the judge's robe erases all sense of family loyalty when judging is to be done? Even if you lose? Not bluddy likely! But that's what the provinces are supposed to swallow.

Probably the most obvious of loaded appointments was when Pierre Trudeau appointed Bora Laskin to be Chief Justice of Canada in 1973. Laskin was a scholar, an academic, and in constitutional terms a "federalist," as indeed most people appointed to the SCC are. But Trudeau, who had constitutional changes in mind such as patriating the constitution from Westminster, knew that Laskin would state the federal case very strongly to his colleagues. Chief Justice Laskin lasted long enough to see Mr. Trudeau's dream of bringing the constitution home with a Charter of Rights and Freedoms attached. Whether that's good or bad or would have happened anyway is beside the point, which is that the judicial arm of our government, like the legislative and executive arms, is controlled by the prime minister. It's true that during his time in office the prime minister won't have anywhere near nine vacancies to fill on the court, but in the course of a long string of power, one party certainly gets to appoint friendly faces to a lot of the judicial armchairs.

Is it possible that a SCC bench appointed by an accepted impartial process would have also decided in favour of Trudeau's constitutional undertakings? Of course it is, but reread Lord Hewart (above).

Perhaps the most obvious "planting" of a friendly voice in the SCC in recent times came in 1997 when, because the prejudices of the man appointed were the same as most of English-speaking Canada at the time, we (excepting me, I might add) overlooked his clear bias. Michel Basterache is an Acadian from New Brunswick and his appointment came at a time when federal politics was all astir about whether or not Quebec could legally secede and, if so, on what terms. There was a vacancy in the SCC Chamber and Jean Chrétien took the opportunity to appoint a francophone not from Quebec, a man who was against Quebec separating. Chrétien, in making the appointment, gave as a reason that Basterache had shown his loyalty to Canada by co-chairing the "Yes" side of the Charlottetown Accord debate. Wait a minute here! This means the millions of Canadians (nearly 70 percent of BC residents) who voted "no" were disloyal! This is a bit much for this Charlottetown opponent to stomach. In any event, the prime minister appointed to the SCC bench a man who was strongly biased on an issue before the Court and because most Canadians agreed with him, somehow the appointment was acceptable. This isn't quite buying a judge but damned near. It is the basic and essential rule that judges bring to the bench not their opinions but their wisdom. It's hard to accept a judge's wisdom before he has even heard the case—there is not that essential appearance of fairness that the most evil of those who appear before him must clearly see.

But the conundrum remains: Someone has to appoint judges but who and under what, if any, constraints? Prime Minister Stephen Harper has an interesting solution—set up a council to advise him then stack the council with faithful Tories and "hang 'em high" reactionaries. Evidently, this is better than Harper just appointing pals. He can always respond to criticism by blaming the appointment on his "impartial" council. (In fact, the minister of justice does the appointing, but I'm sure I needn't remind you of who appoints the minister of justice.)

What about the US system where the president's nominations to high courts must be approved by the Senate, which has the right to hold probing and sometimes highly political hearings? Many Canadians don't like the open politics of that system. I think it's fine to make candidates demonstrate their fitness for office, but I'm clearly in a minority.

Not for the first time, British Columbia leads the way with a highly workable system for appointing Provincial Court judges. First off, lawyers apply for the job and lay their careers out for inspection by the Judicial Council of British Columbia, which is made up of nine members as designated by section 21(2) of the Provincial Court Act. The chief judge is the presiding member or chair, with an associate chief judge as alternate presiding member. The attorney general appoints four lay members, one of which is traditionally a judicial justice of the peace and by strong tradition all are non-political. The remaining members of the Judicial Council are the president of the Provincial Court Judges Association, the president (or a designate) of the BC Branch of the Canadian Bar Association, and a lawyer appointed by the Law Society of BC. This council recommends candidates to the cabinet, which has the last word, and while that makes it a political decision, notice the fine, though hugely important line between the *political leader submitting a nomination and an independent council recommending one.* There is no reason whatever why a similar process could not apply to federal appointments, not just to the Supreme Court of Canada but to the Federal Court, Provincial Supreme and Appeal Courts.

It won't happen because Stephen Harper wants to load the

Supreme Court of Canada with—frankly—friendly right wing Tories. We all remember how a Republican Supreme Court of the United States abandoned ancient precedents and with hopelessly twisted logic made George W. Bush president over Al Gore. It's this power over the top court that Harper covets. If the system is reformed by having a "loaded" council, the selection will always be the prime minister's, which is to say always political. On the other hand, under the British Columbia system it's the Council that makes the recommendation and, while cabinet still has the final say-so, to refuse such a candidate, except in the case of an obvious bad decision, would take more political courage than most cabinets could muster. On that point and to sum up, when I was in cabinet, the son of a Dave Barrett cabinet minister—one the Socreds particularly disliked—came forward for our consideration. There were some rumblings to be sure, but none of us wanted to be seen nixing a Judicial Council recommendation because of raw partisanship. He was immediately appointed.

Ottawa should look to British Columbia for guidance, but to do so would break a long tradition of rejecting anything Ottawa didn't think of first, especially if it arises west of the Rockies.

Quebec, Who Needs It?

No one can predict with certainty what would happen if Quebec left Canada, an event that in itself that would cause huge strains. One can only say Canada would be very different without its principal raison d'être. It's hard to see how it could keep going without massive changes to our style of governance. Yet instead of quietly preparing alternatives, Prime Minister Harper seems hell-bent on a policy of appeasing Quebec, the notion that she is a "nation" being the most harmful suggestion since Brian Mulroney invented "distinct society." The fact that Harper is dead wrong and has made a huge mistake is proved beyond doubt by the fact that the mainstream media support him in it.

The *Globe and Mail*'s Jeffrey Simpson, however, has it right. What do the words mean? If they mean something, tell us; if they mean nothing, why put them into the political mix? But alas for Mr. Harper and a triple alas for Canada, these words do mean something. The only question to be answered is "What is the precise definition?" Whether it's "sovereignty-association," "distinct society" or

"Québécois Nation," one must summon up the guru of matters of this sort, Humpty Dumpty:

> "When I use a word," Humpty Dumpty said, in a rather scornful tone, "it means just what I choose it to mean—neither more nor less."
>
> "The question is," said Alice, "whether you can make words mean so many different things."
>
> "The question is," said Humpty Dumpty, "which is to be master. That's all."

There will be no instant event. We will, as Churchill said, "be adamant for drift." "Drifting" is a Canadian national characteristic. Interestingly, Harper says he made the motion in order to help Jean Charest, premier of Quebec, in his election on March 26, 2007. Any prime minister who tried that in BC would be tarred and feathered and ridden out of town on a rail!

However, the insidious thing is that the word "nation," whether applied to the Québécois or Quebec is the last step before another separation move. Mr. Harper has done this country great, irreparable damage. Canada cannot exist without Quebec and we should understand that. We should also understand that Humpty Dumpty was right so that Mr. Harper's definition will surely be different than that of Quebeckers, especially Quebec sovereigntists.

On Healthcare

As the politicians fall all over their tongues saying that Medicare is sacred, Canadians find themselves with a publicly financed healthcare system that is like your old car—it's not worth fixing but it's all the transportation you have. The healthcare system's broke because no government has dared grasp the nettle and reform it so that expenditures match the new realities; that, you see, would alienate the very powerful groups who hitherto have had most of the Medicare pie.

Medicare is driven by the medical profession. In general it can be said that the fees for almost all the illnesses that need curing are paid to doctors out of Medicare while the fees for virtually all preventative measures are not. Thus, the incentive for the medical doctor is to cure, not prevent. In fact, the real experts in both prevention and non-intrusive healing fall outside the medical profession, but doctors see any support for alternative care as an attack on their share of the health dollars. And the system is so deeply entrenched that a major issue, mental health, gets scant attention because governments don't want to find out more about it for fear of the expense of treatment.

The 1986 Canada Health Act accepted the status quo, meaning that Medicare remains essentially a drug and surgery system where the more visits and procedures, the more money is paid to the doctors. The best way to accommodate this would be to pay each doctor a yearly stipend for looking after patients without worrying about what he did for them. This is called the "capitation" method and, for obvious reasons, doctors hate it.

But as the person in charge at Medicare, how could you tell if doctors were charging for too many visits unless the abuse was flagrant? How could you say that a referral wasn't needed? As a Medicare watchdog, how could you be sure that the batch of expensive procedures the doctor ordered were all necessary? And from the doctor's point of view, what can you do when a patient insists on a MRI scan even though you don't think it necessary?

Let's look at what has happened to this doctor-driven system in the last twenty-five years. In 1980 when I was BC health minister, no one had heard of AIDS, there were no organ transplants and while there were a few scanners about, MRI had not arrived. Nor had the "Boomers" reached the age where they became expensive to keep well. In 1980 healthcare consumed about 22 percent of BC's budget; it's now 44 percent and expected to go over 60 percent in the next decade. During this same period the federal government drastically reduced transfer payments as Paul Martin balanced his budget on the backs of the ill. Meanwhile, the BC NDP have criticized the Liberal government's failure to add five thousand new long-term care beds, ignoring the fact that the high number of beds now needed is in large part because of NDP neglect. Since 1980, therefore, we have incurred huge medical obligations, the vast majority of which are reposed in a system that places a high priority on treatment with, at best, token attention to prevention.

The problem is this: When an obese person sees a dietician early—at his own expense—he avoids the ailments the untreated obese person will get and he doesn't become a permanent fixture in the doctor's office, resulting in bills to Medicare. What cannot be quantified is the effect of that dietician's labours to prevent his obesity because neither the dietician nor the patient are in the system. And there is the rub. Politicians are involved in two timelines, one being the next election and the other the budgetary benefits that must come in the same fiscal year the expenses were incurred. It's a Catch-22 where you could vastly improve the health of many people, thus lowering health costs, but you can't get the money to do that until this better health has arrived! And this is why we are locked into a healthcare system that pays huge bucks for treatment and almost nothing for prevention, which would have saved us much of those large bucks paid out for treatment!

Another persistent and dangerous outgrowth of our present system is the wait-list for surgery. Our governments have made some progress in reducing waiting time but not as much as they say they have, for while the *percentages* look impressive, the actual days involved are still unacceptable. Try 250 days for cataract surgery (especially since you've probably reached your later years), 92 days for an MRI, joint replacements in 9 to 12 months and so on.

What no government will admit, being in fear of Medicare's sainted founder, Tommy Douglas, his ghost and his daughter Shirley, is that we can no longer afford all the healthcare Canadians want out of public funds. Governments will try to look as if they are covering all the bases by throwing some cash into the pot from time to time but it will never be enough. In fact, all it does is push down a bump on the pie plate, which causes another bump to pop up. Sooner or later we will be forced to give some room to private money or ration services—or both.

Healthcare is like a besieged castle. As the enemy keeps pounding on the gates, the leader within cries out, "Be of stout heart! There can't be many more of them!" Yet the siege continues and, rather than fewer enemies, they seem to increase exponentially. The leader is then faced with a dilemma: Either he comes to terms or he loses all. The worst of it is that the leader has never used his best weapons, such as building battlements away from the fortress to prevent the enemy from getting close to it in the first place. I admit that my metaphor is strained yet it's perfectly valid. As the cost of healthcare moves past 50 percent of provincial budgets, those governments will have to do something drastic. When they see that doing their own thing by making a deal with private money still leaves them ahead of the game even after the federal government has taken away their transfer payments, they will go it alone.

Saying and wishing that isn't so doesn't alter the fact that it is.

PART IV

Freedoms, Rights and Privileges

Media Censorship

"These are the times that try men's souls." Thus Tom Paine started a series of pamphlets which helped inspire and sustain the American Revolution. At the time the mainstream media were subject to British censorship but Paine, a brave man, found a way around it.

In the '30s Winston Churchill and several other MPs tried to warn the government about Hitler. The British press refused to cover the issue and the BBC refused to give Churchill airtime. We know what happened. Here is what a later critic had to say: "It is hard to censor the press when it wants to be free, but easy if it gives up its freedom easily."

We often hear about the freedoms our forebears fought and died for ... but it's just a phrase that rolls off the tongue with little if any thought. I recommend to you a book called *Towards the Light* by A.C. Grayling, an English professor and constant champion of rights. Read this and you'll have some idea of just what sacrifices were made and just what we seem hell-bent to sacrifice.

There is no government censor at work in Canada, and that is because the government doesn't need one. Look at some events of the past fifteen years. Remember the Charlottetown Accord referendum where 55 percent of Canadians and 70 percent of British Columbians turned it down? Every single establishment media outlet, far from examining the issue carefully, fell in line with Prime Minister Mulroney, and one of the largest of them, Maclean-Hunter, actually signed in on the "Yes" side. There was one exception—a talk-show host at CKNW who will go unnamed. And who broke the story of the graft and corruption of the Mulroney years? It sure as hell wasn't the media. It was the ever-courageous Stevie Cameron, blacklisted by the establishment media.

Then we have the sordid picture of Brian Mulroney accepting $300,000 in cash from Mr. Fixit of the Airbus scandal, Karlheinz Schreiber. It took thirteen *years* after this happened for CBC's *Fifth Estate* to blow the whistle. Where was the establishment media on this? Protecting the ass of a member of the establishment, that's where.

Closer to home, it took an independent journalist, Sean Holman, to finally crack the Doug Walls case, he being the accused fraud artist whom Premier Campbell put in charge of approximately $500 million assigned to the Ministry of Children and Families. In a teeth-pulling exercise, the premier first told Holman that he had never heard of Walls; when it became clear that Walls' wife was Mrs. Campbell's cousin, Campbell replied, "So what? My wife has too many cousins to keep track of them all." Further prodding got the premier to admit that he did know Walls; he then admitted he had been a house guest of the Walls family then finally confessed that he had gone all the way to Prince George to lease a car from Mr. Walls. All this was uncovered by the persistence of one independent journalist, not the establishment media.

We live in an era where the president of the United States and the prime minister of Great Britain baldly lied about Iraq having weapons of mass destruction. We have a US president who holds hostages just as the Taliban—and for that matter, the State of Israel—does; a US president who approves of torturing; a US president who openly says he won't obey the law of the land if he thinks it interferes with his role as commander-in-chief. In Canada we have a government that muzzles its MPs, refuses to answer questions and takes its marching orders from those who think God talks to them. And the establishment media says nothing.

Why is the media behaving thus? In part it's because the papers own most of the radio and TV stations and don't want to raise the ire of the licensing authority, the CRTC, which is, of course, the government's poodle. Partly it's because historically in this country the establishment media looks after its own because it is itself part of that establishment. The talent to muckrake—which, incidentally, is an honourable term with a long history of uncovering graft and corruption—is there, but what good is that if these reporters can't get it printed or on the airwaves?

In fairness, I can't remember any time that there has been an aggressive media in this province or this country. Back when I was a lad, newspapers were either Liberal (the *Vancouver Sun*) or Conservative (the *Vancouver Province*). As far as the *Toronto Globe and Mail* and other "eastern" papers were concerned, western Canada was waves of wheat fields with God-only-knows-what on the west side of the Rockies. It's just not in our tradition to have hard journalism interfere with what our constitution calls "peace, order and good government."

This is why internet papers like thetyee.ca and Opinion250.com, both of which I write for, are increasingly being read by those who care for uncensored news and opinions.

Thomas Jefferson said, "The basis of our governments being the opinion of the people, the very first object should be to keep that right; and were it left to me to decide whether we should have a government without newspapers or newspapers without a government, I should not hesitate a moment to prefer the latter." While that stand might seem extravagant for 2007, it puts into clear focus the fact that a country cannot be truly free if its media are manacled either by a government or on its own initiative.

Given the pathetic media we have, is it any wonder we have such terrible governments?

The Freedom to Insult

I was inspired by an article in *The Guardian Weekly* some months ago on the "Struggle for Free Speech," written by Timothy Garton Ash, a widely read political writer whose byline often appears in the local press. He points out that free speech is under attack all over the world including, sadly, the birthplaces and repositories of that notion, Britain and America. If we were important enough to be noticed, he could have added Canada as well.

I think the issue of restriction of free speech can be divided into three areas, which often slop over into one another. First, there is that speech that incites violence. I know of no one who would argue that "Kill the Jews" or "Let's destroy a Sikh temple" qualifies as free speech. What is troubling, of course, is those who use free speech tendentiously by cloaking themselves in words of liberty while any reasonable inference to be drawn from their words cries out for violence. The old "For God's sake, don't throw him in the duck pond!" sort of speech. This area demands much more space than I have here, but even with this kind of language I would err on the side of free speech if only because the late Doug Collins, James Keegstra and Ernst Zündel couldn't have survived without the publicity given them by the media after the well-meaning howls of anguish from groups like the Canadian Jewish Congress.

Second, there is the matter of criticism of authority. In the United States under the rule of the Solomon v. *New York Times* case, damages will not be given a "public figure" against a critic unless the words were not only wrong but also *harmful and malicious*. This rule doesn't apply in the UK and Canada, meaning that people in power here do very well indeed in defamation suits. They also employ the friendly law as "libel chill," which manifests itself in a public figure letting it be known that if the media pursues his affairs any further he'll sue them for libel. It's a very effective weapon, but since you can't quantify a negative there's no way of knowing just how effective.

Third, there is the insult, an almost a dead art because of political correctness spawned by an unrestricted zeal not only to curtail that which might encourage violence but to prevent hurting anyone's feelings. Here we find ourselves being censured by the "proper" sort of people (in the late Denny Boyd's wonderful phrase, "higher purpose persons") and censored by a media that is afraid to offend. Far too often that fear of offending isn't just because the average Canadian is afraid to go outside the bounds of political correctness as it is the media's kow-towing to politicians (about which more in a moment).

We must bring back the decent insult. Once an art form, the insult was perfected, of course, by Churchill. Speaking in the Commons, he looked at Prime Minister Ramsay MacDonald and said, "I remember when I was a child, being taken to the celebrated Barnum's circus, the exhibit on the program which I most desired to see was the one described as 'The Boneless Wonder.' My parents judged that that spectacle would be too revolting and demoralizing for my youthful eyes, [and] I have waited fifty years to see the boneless wonder sitting on the Treasury Bench." He also said of MacDonald that he had, "more than any other man, the gift of compressing the largest amount of words into the smallest amount of thought," a jibe that has also been attributed to Lincoln. One night at dinner he was seated next to the formidable Labour MP Bessie Braddock with whom he got into a heated exchange. Exasperated, she said, "Sir, you are drunk."

"Madam, you are ugly," Churchill replied. "In the morning I shall be sober."

He once said of Clement Attlee that he was a "modest little man with a great deal to be modest about." (He denied saying this, but it's a hell of a good insult and Churchillian to the core.)

John Montagu, Earl of Sandwich, once said to that great beacon of free speech, John Wilkes, "Egad, sir, I do not know whether you will die on the gallows or of the pox."

Wilkes replied, "That will depend, my lord, on whether I embrace your principles or your mistress."

The great barrister F.E. Smith (later the 1st Lord Birkenhead) was deliciously rude to judges. On one occasion he and opposing counsel were having a set-to when the judge said, "There, there, gentlemen, why do you think I'm here?" To which Smith replied, "It's not for me to explain the divine workings of Providence." During another case the judge looked down at Smith and said, "I've read your brief and am none the wiser." "Perhaps not," replied Smith, "but much better informed."

So where is all this going? you might ask.

Our liberties, especially since 9/11, are being systematically eroded by a government bent on protecting us by, for example, banishing nail clippers and small tubes of Krazy Glue from airplanes. (Yes, that happened to me, making me wonder if I looked like someone who would run through the cabin brandishing a one-inch nail file while shouting "Death to the infidels!" then Krazy Gluing the pilot to his chair.)

But the bigger threat by far is the media. Ownership of many radio stations and all TV networks by the same people who own the newspaper chains means that newspapers, for the first time in this country, must be nice to the government or risk losing or not being granted their licences to broadcast or telecast. This means that virtually all media outlets in Canada pull their punches when dealing with government. Thus, freedom of the press is circumscribed by rules that don't need to be stated but which result in criticism of the government being blunted by the practical need for government largesse.

We have wound up with an anally retentive country that gets only censored news and, to make matters infinitely worse, censors itself for fear of being seen as politically incorrect. We are a nation of pussy-footers and, sad to say, we may like it that way. Where we once had people like Marjorie Nichols, Allan Fotheringham, Jack Webster, Pat Burns, Ed Murphy, Jack Wasserman, a full-time Jim Hume and Allen Garr on the provincial scene and, dare I say it, Rafe Mair, truly holding Victoria's feet to the fire, we now have on-the-one-hand/on-the-other-hand radio and a print media that is but a shadow of its former self. Canada has "free speech" provided that it falls within the boundaries of what the establishment considers reasonable dissent. In that world there is no place for courageous journalism and we should all understand that.

The Freedom to
Willfully Promote Hatred

Question: Why is Ernst Zündel in a German prison and David Irving in an Austrian one?

Answer: Because both those countries, based on well-justified national shame, make it against the criminal law to deny the Holocaust. Surely this is unacceptable. In Canada I can deny that there was a Second World War, that Sir John A. Macdonald was ever a prime minister of Canada or pronounce moon shots faked and insist that the earth is flat. My only punishment would be that I would rightly be seen as a kook. I can deny that any Canadians died at Dieppe, deny that Hong Kong Canadian defenders were imprisoned in ghastly Japanese prisons or that Pol Pot all but exterminated the people of Cambodia. Now I become a kook that has insulted the memories of literally millions of people. But I don't go to jail because in Canada we still have some, though it's dwindling, free speech. Of course, the evidence of the Holocaust is incontrovertible (as are the other events cited above), mainly in large part because the Nazis kept meticulous records of what they did.

All accept that free speech is not an absolute right. It can be constrained in times of war, for example. It also must be restrained if it used to incite violence against a person or persons or any identifiable group. But, as always, the devil is in the details. How do you go far enough without going too far?

Section 319 (2) of the Criminal Code of Canada makes it a crime to communicate, except in private conversation, statements that *willfully promote hatred* against an identifiable group (my emphasis). The courts have had difficulty with these words. Surely it's not trite to point out that political parties do exactly that all the time. So do the sports fans who cheer on the local ruffian on the ice every time he provokes a fight. It's little wonder that the courts, mandated to find guilt beyond a reasonable doubt, have difficulty finding guilt unless it's clear that the accused not only produced "hate literature" but intended it to do specific harm to a specific group. It must be noted, too, that the courts have held that "willfully" does not include "recklessly." And parliaments always have trouble when they try to pronounce upon public morality. And that's what we're dealing with here for the most part. We are attempting to legislate against bad manners, hurtful speech and terrible insults.

The stand I take is not new: I believe in free speech even when it hurts people's feelings, even badly. It's hard to imagine any uncomplimentary remark that couldn't be construed by some as preaching harm to the object of the remark. Indeed, as I mentioned, things as common as sporting events and political campaigns automatically include intemperate statements that could easily be construed as calling for bodily harm and worse. But the slur, the gross insult, the expressions of prejudice all belong in the sphere of human expression that must be dealt with by the disapproval of decent people, not the courts—societal discipline, not criminal lawsuits.

What the law is aiming for, I think, is criminalizing serious calls for harm to be done. "Let's go burn down the synagogue" and that sort of thing clearly must be proscribed by law and prosecuted vigorously. Surely all decent people should agree with that. The trouble is the law goes too far when it says one must not *willfully promote hatred against an identifiable group*. If the term "physical harm" were to replace "hatred" that would cover the situation we're trying to deal with, but I suspect that wouldn't satisfy the Canadian Jewish Congress and similar groups.

The infamous Ernst Zündel underwent two criminal trials—1985 and 1988—in Canada. The Crown, knowing that it would be tough to make Section 319 of the Criminal Code stick, chose lesser charges under Section 180, alleging that he "did publish a statement or tale, namely, "Did Six Million Really Die?" that he knows is false and that is likely to cause mischief to the public interest in social and racial tolerance, contrary to the Criminal Code." Zündel was originally found guilty by two juries but was finally acquitted by the Supreme Court of Canada which held in 1992 that section 180 was a violation of the guarantees of freedom of expression under the Canadian Charter of Rights and Freedoms and the section was struck down as unconstitutional. So if this "easier" section was unconstitutional, it's safe to infer that Section 319 is also all but unenforceable.

David Irving, acknowledged as a brilliant researcher, has been rightly and roundly criticized for apologizing for Hitler and the Nazi regime, for his hatred of Jews and his denial of the Holocaust—and for writing rubbish about Churchill! It was he, you may remember, who exposed "the Hitler Diaries" as frauds, thus greatly embarrassing the famous British historian Hugh Trevor-Roper (Lord Dacre) who had confirmed them as being legitimate.

Unfortunately, Irving is also a neo-Nazi, a devoted hater of Jews and a denier of the Holocaust. In the "what goes around comes around department" Irving sued the American writer Deborah Lipstadt and Penguin Books for libel, got soundly thrashed and was left broke with 175,000 pounds in legal costs he must pay the defendants, plus what must have been astronomical fees to his barristers.

What is of considerable interest and supports my thesis is the position Ms. Lipstadt, a Jew, now takes viv-a-vis Mr. Irving: "In the

United States, the First Amendment guarantees people a right to make total fools of themselves. Sometimes it is painful to hear, but I would rather they had the freedom to say what they wished than the government had the power to control them."

There is no doubt that both Zündel and Irving carefully calculated to deeply wound Jewish sensibilities and there can be no doubt that both are vicious anti-Semites. But they are not in jail because they tried to incite violence but because of their idiotic denial of the Holocaust.

Freedom of speech should never be diminished to make prosecutions easier. The fact that in Canada Zündel escaped the consequences of his filthy mind and actions tells me that Canadians are much inclined to regard freeing people like that as the insurance premium free people pay for the preservation of that freedom.

Youth Gangs

Much has rightly been made of the number and activities of youth gangs. What is not remembered is that they've been around for a long time, as Leonard Bernstein's *West Side Story* attests. There were gangs in Vancouver when I grew up. Moreover, when I was a kid, Hallowe'en was a nightmare with virtually every policeman on the streets. Cars were overturned, buildings burned, fences knocked down—you name it.

In more recent times the youth gangs in large cities have often been ethnic. In New York City, Italian, black and Puerto Rican gangs are, or at least have been, prevalent. Now we see Asian gangs in Vancouver. I'm not sloughing this problem off because it's common but only making the point that there's some history here. And at the same time we shouldn't forget that the worst of all gangs are the biker groups like the Hell's Angels and they are mostly Caucasians.

The reasons that ethnic gangs are formed are many, but through my dealings with guests who know about these things I learned that the major one is protection of their ethnic group from active racism. Again, I don't make light of this. Nothing justifies the gangs we have in our community, but what I am saying is that society can make a difference by finding ways to reduce racial discrimination. On the other hand, the gang itself is not the real problem. What *is* the problem is the criminality that finds its home in the gangs. This is an important point for it tells us that the issue in large part belongs to the ethnic community. Too often parents in an ethnic community set out codes of behaviour that are very difficult for their youth, growing up in a much different society, to accept. The second and third generations are not interested in things like arranged marriages or the political problems "back home," so to find sanctuary from the community and modern Metro Vancouver society, a gang seems the only place to go. It's just too easy for an Asian community to say, "This is our culture and we want to bring our children up in it." When newcomers arrive on our shores, they know what the social mores are.

It's equally counterproductive for the Caucasian community to lay the problem at the ethnic community by saying, "These Asian kids are all the same. Being brutal in gangs comes naturally to them and is encouraged by their elders." It takes bridges that are built to deal with the problem, and while I know much is being done, much more must be done so that all communities can come to grips with the problems. I'm as troubled by this situation as anybody, but we can't go back because this is the hand we've been dealt and we must play it.

The first observation I would make is that most new immigrant groups tend to stick together and thus they are seen as unwelcome newcomers. One only has to think of the Irish and the Italians in New York who, to stereotype, became policemen or crooks and sometimes both. At the same time we must remember that it's very natural for birds of a feather to stick together; in fact, the all-time prize for "clannishness" goes to the British in the places they colonized.

The second observation is that white people tend to blend into white communities because it's so easy. Usually there are commonalities of religion and culture so that the addition of newcomers, while not seamless, is easier than with "coloured" groups. Following that thought, it's easier and safer for coloured immigrants to stick together and help each other—and maintain their own discrete community. This is true of coloured citizens of many generations. And if there is little intermarriage with whites, it keeps the community strong, if inward-looking. On the other hand, many white communities—the Jews and Greeks come readily to mind—wish to keep cohesive communities, too, and put barriers up against intermarriage.

The third observation is that coloured immigrants will often do the jobs that the white community doesn't want to do and this causes clashes at the lower end of the wage scale.

It's not my intention here to blame the white majority for the sin of prejudice. As with all things, there are at least two sides to the question. The Indo-Canadian community has its problems with violence and lawlessness among their young; they know this and are, as a community, addressing it. And this is where the partial answer to the problem (there never will be a complete one) lies. Communities must reach out to others, a responsibility devolved on all of us. We are social animals and differences between clans are bound to be irritating. Minimizing those differences is the only path to reasonable relations between groups of fellow Canadians.

Too Young

As a general rule I place the musings of insurance companies right up there with Pinocchio when his nose reached its longest. Especially, I have little if any regard for the musings of Allstate for whom I once worked as an adjustor and that later was an occasional client of my law firm. Allstate was dubbed "All Heart" by those who had a claim only to have their insurance cancelled or those who were at the business end of a claim against the company. But here is a quote from an Allstate official that caught my eye in an editorial in *The Economist* not long ago: "A sixteen-year-old can't see an NC-17 rated movie, drink alcohol or vote. But drive a 5,000-pound car at 60 mph? That's OK."

Allstate has a point, a very good point. The evidence of teenage recklessness seems to be a daily headline. Young kids racing; two people dead. Senior killed by hit-and-run young driver. On and bloody (literally) on it goes. The police are driven to distraction by this epidemic and spend far too much of their time on it. For example, every time there's a hit-and-run accident the police must investigate, taking them away from other duties, meaning that teenage accidents compel a use of police time that would be much better spent on other matters. Courts seem loath to give out severe sentences and find that, like the police, a disproportionate amount of time is spent on cases that wouldn't happen if the age one can get a driver's licence were extended to nineteen. The blows to the family, friends and communities are hard and the pain runs deep. As a father who lost a seventeen-year-old daughter due to reckless driving (her own), I know about the pain and what it so tragically does to the security of the affected family.

I'm not one of those who looks back to my teenage days as unblemished by any stupid behaviour. Far from it. I got my licence when I was sixteen and was technically a good driver (the inspector said my reactions were in the top 10 percent), but I had little fear and almost no judgment. I was involved in several accidents but fortunately no one was hurt. We had drag races and often played "tag" with another car, the object being to lose him. Up and down lanes and busy streets we went. What fun it was, especially when homeowners, pedestrians and other drivers shook their fists at us. I had no business having a driver's licence nor did 75 percent of my friends. (That figure would be higher today because, when I was a kid, girls drove much more safely than boys, a difference that no longer exists.)

We kids didn't hesitate for a moment just because we had been drinking. In fact, that was the situation most of the times we got behind the wheel with our parents' car full of our teenage friends. Other drugs weren't fashionable in those days but with the amount of booze we drank it didn't matter. On a Monday morning when, just before school went in, we were having a cigarette down the alley, you could depend upon one kid telling how shit-faced he had been on Saturday night, only to be matched by an even more hair-raising story.

It seems to me we must ask ourselves a question: Is a driver's licence a right or a privilege? Actually the answer is easy. The courts have long held that it's a privilege. Now comes the harder question: Do we extend that privilege to people as soon as they are big enough to drive a car? The answer is no because there are lots of kids of twelve who are big enough. It must be then that we grant the licence when a person is mature enough, and we've arbitrarily decided that this happens on the sixteenth birthday. We ought to have our collective heads read.

Of course, there are some very responsible drivers under the age of nineteen and it would be unfair to take away their right—I mean, privilege—to drive. But who ever said life would be fair? And is it really that unfair? We set all sorts of rules so we can have an orderly society. And remember that here we're talking about a society extending a privilege. Surely that society is entitled to say, "We know that many young drivers are good and we also know that many older drivers are terrible, but the issue is public safety and we know that a hugely disproportionate number of injuries and deaths on the road are caused by drivers under nineteen." To argue that other drivers are bad too is a diversion, not an argument.

Move the age for a driver's licence to nineteen when other perks and responsibilities of adults are granted. This may require a special "when driving during employment" exception. So be it. Let everyone else wait until adulthood to exercise a very important privilege— driving a car and doing so carefully.

On Veiled Ladies

I just don't see where this fuss about Muslim women wearing a full veil is getting us, and frankly, as Clark Gable said at the end of *Gone With the Wind*, I just don't give a damn.

In Britain the main fuss occurred in 2006 over a teaching assistant in full veil. The matter was referred to whatever council it is that hears these things and, while they gave the lady a thousand quid for her embarrassment, they said she would have to take off her veil while teaching. It seems that the main issue in the school's approach was that the veil acts as a divider between one culture and another. If that's really the case, it's a bit late. Britons should have thought of that long ago as a reason for not taking people from the far-flung regions of the "Empah" into their country.

At this writing there is much angst and political turmoil over women who seek to vote wearing veils. Isn't all this just a bit racist, like the now forgotten fuss in Canadian Legions about allowing men wearing turbans in on Remembrance Day? Don't we all remember the unctuous and tendentious arguments that the Legion presented that no one must be permitted to show disrespect for the Queen by wearing headgear? Nothing to do with prejudice against ragheads . . . oops! Indo-Canadian gentlemen! Perish the thought!

Why don't we go after other indicia of difference? I knew a man in London who had gone to Harrow and even in his sixties was always seen in a Harrow school tie. It was stained with food and beer droppings from the past and the present, but that tie was always there, a sign of social if not monetary superiority. Lapel pins are another way to tell people how you are different. Perhaps all members of the armed forces should be stripped of their stripes and ribbons so there would be no outward distinction between them and non-commissioned officers.

There is this consideration too: In declaiming against veils people create an issue where there wasn't one until they spoke out. Don't we have bigger, better and more serious issues to trouble ourselves with?

They Protesteth Too Much

The 2006 Muslim reaction to the insulting Danish cartoons is interesting because it not only places in contrast western values of free speech with the censorship of most Muslim countries, but it also confirms a certain hypocrisy—at least in the political arm of Islam. We in the West believe in free speech, which includes the right to be rude, disrespectful and downright nasty, In fact, without the right to insult, free speech wouldn't mean much. Hypocrisy comes in the way many Muslim cartoonists caricature Jews as beak-nosed, slimy-looking money lenders, while the Muslim leadership is silent.

Political cartoons are supposed to be hard-edged. That's their whole point. If they incite violence against someone, that's another thing. That must be punished. There are over a billion Muslims in the world and it would be wrong to think that most of them support violence. The fact is, however, a hell of a lot of them do, and if that fact cannot be conveyed by cartoons, which always exaggerate to make the point, we place ourselves in the position of most Muslim states—without free speech.

On Jesus and Mohammed

W e are supposed to be in a godless age. The only god we accept is Mammon. But if so, how come we have two religions, each divided within their own ranks but apparently bent on having a mutual Armageddon? It's nearly 2,000 years since Jesus was with us and nearly 1,500 since Mohammed, like Jesus, was taken away bodily to heaven, and if anything, the hostility is more severe than ever.

This shouldn't surprise us because both religions and ethnicities, bearing grudges, bear them forever. Look at the Balkans. Even with several religions and ethnic groups, Yugoslavia under Tito was peaceful and relatively prosperous. Shortly after strongman Tito died, the various ethnic and religious communities were literally at each other's throats. Iraq, since the downfall of its vicious strongman Saddam Hussein, has been fractured into three warring factions, two of them on the religion question. And much of Christian America eagerly awaits the big battle.

How ironic it is that two men of peace, Jesus and Mohammed, have left such a horrible legacy of followers who would like nothing more than to kill each other.

PART V

Closer to Home

Harriet Nahanee Did Not Die in Vain

The Eagleridge Bluffs case is well known. Put simply, the BC government is building a bridge over the Sea-to-Sky Highway at Eagleridge Bluffs so the route to Whistler can bypass the traffic that uses Horseshoe Bay as a major ferry terminal. The Coalition to Save Eagleridge Bluffs, largely made up of citizens from the area—three piece suit protesters and pearl necklaces abounding—protested and indeed had sit-ins aimed at forcing the government to proceed by tunnel, thus saving this unique and highly sensitive area from the front-end loaders and gravel trucks. They proved, if proof is necessary, that all protesters are not rheumy-eyed, unkempt haired and string-bearded apparitions from the "left." Quite clearly, on the evidence, a slightly more expensive tunnel (probably not more expensive if all issues are counted) would have been much better for motorists and residents alike. But I'm not going to deal with the merits here, though I support the Coalition. I'm going to try to analyze what this decision means.

Perhaps the least important result is that the mayor of the District of West Vancouver, Pamela Goldsmith-Jones, will likely not be re-elected after she first supported the Coalition then, after pressure from the provincial government, did a turnabout. Of much more serious consequence was the death of Native elder Harriet Nahanee, aged seventy-one, after being sent to jail for refusing to apologize for her contempt of court. I don't believe it's a stretch to conclude that Ms. Nahanee, not well at the time, died because she was sent to Surrey Pretrial Centre, a prison for men and a noted hellhole for women in poor health.

Another woman and a veteran environmentalist, seventy-eight-year-old Betty Krawczyk, was sentenced to ten months imprisonment for contempt of court for her non-violent passive resistance at the construction site. More about this later.

I have spoken to leaders of the Coalition and they have accepted defeat only because the government and the construction company have unbeatable legal tools at hand. Although it's doubtful that the Coalition will continue their actions when the Olympics arrive, they have not lost their anger and are looking for ways to help other communities with similar problems to the ones they faced. In fact, at a huge protest in the East Delta Agricultural Hall I would guess that fully one-third of the packed house came from West Vancouver. Radical left wing speakers included Gordon Price, former NPA councillor in Vancouver; Delta councillor Vicki Huntington who shares the politics of her late father who was a Tory MP and cabinet minister; John Cummins, a current Tory MP from Delta; and a former Socred minister (no prizes for guessing who!).

What comes out of this sad affair is that there is no *fair* environmental assessment process. There is a process, the outcomes of which average about 98 percent in favour of the government. This is not surprising since the assessor is employed by the government after political appointment by the premier and cabinet.

There are public meetings, which are designed to inform the public, but as anyone who lives in my village of Lions Bay can tell you, these are masterpieces of obfuscation, dissembling and arrogance. The plain, simple and incontrovertible fact is that this, like other similar projects, was a done deal when it was announced, and any attempts to talk to the public thereafter were exercises in deception.

This will surprise you: The Coalition couldn't get the ear of Highways Minister Kevin Falcon who, since he had no intention of changing his plans no matter what the evidence, would not have been any help even had he taken the time to listen. In short, first make the decision, second employ the contractors, lastly consult the people. Ready, Fire, Aim! The Liberal MLA, Joan McIntyre, was no use at all since the only MLAs with less clout than those in the opposition side are those from the government backbenches. When I have written in the past in thetyee.ca and in my books that under our system MLAs and MPs are powerless ciphers, I've often been called cynical. Well, here is a classic example of the ineffectiveness of the local member of the legislative assembly. A fencepost with hair could hardly be of less use.

Let us now get back to Harriet Nahanee and Betty Krawczyk, one who died as a result of being in prison and the other jailed for ten months, both sent to the slammer for contempt of court. We all agree that court orders must be obeyed if the rule of law is to prevail. But what if the court allows itself to be used as the strong arm of government and big business by making a civil matter into a crime? *What if government and big business can operate irrespective of public opinion and without having to obtain fair legitimacy for their projects while those who protest go into the slammer?* Because that's the real question here, and it takes those of a certain age back to the bad old days of labour-management relations where union leaders were constantly jailed for contempt because they disobeyed a court order made unfairly—that is, unfairly in the sense that all the legal tools had been given to management. After government finally came to its senses, a Labour Code was enacted and a Labour Relations Board set up so that the playing field was level and workers could see that even if they lost, it had been a fair fight. Relative labour peace without violence and jail terms resulted.

In the case of Eagleridge Bluffs and other cases like it, the order or law being enforced has been passed without a *fair* hearing. People see land they love torn to rat shit without any independent, fair process. What option does that leave those who feel aggrieved by this blatant cloaking a dictatorial diktat in democratic clothing? Of course, they can always pack up and go home, but is that the sort of citizenry Canadians are to become—people who pack up and go home when they have been unfairly dealt with?

There is a lesson to be drawn from all this. Relatively minor abuses of the environment, such as the one at Eagleridge Bluffs, are easily dealt with by a rapacious, unfeeling government. But these "relatively minor" abuses add up to catastrophe. The oceans didn't become close to fishless because of one minor environmental sin but by the accumulation of many. Moreover, all these rapes of the environment had to be approved, or ignored, by government. This case, and uncountable similar examples around the world, show that governments and their industrial partners learned the old lesson well: *Divide and conquer.*

The problem is not a shortage of brave people to protest, it's that they are divided into small groups with no contact with one another. And governments love it that way. One only need look at the deplorable situation in the West Coast fishery to see how government finances large numbers of interest groups to keep them all concentrating on areas of their own special concern rather than presenting a united solid group always in fighting trim.

Eagleridge Bluff makes this point forcefully. Residents and other interested folks could not even stop a project where there was an environmentally sound alternative available. But what if there had been a province-wide coalition for the government to deal with? What if the political fallout wasn't only on one mayor, an MLA or an MP but on all MLAs, MPs, plus mayors and councils? What if the protesters at Eagleridge Bluffs had been supported by the physical presence of hundreds from around the province?

Wouldn't work? Too unwieldy? Maybe so. But considering the way high-handed governments are pushing us around now, surely that's worth a try? When your mayor won't support you, when your MLA won't support you, when your government won't support you, when you are sent to jail for protesting a decision based on a phony environmental process, what are you to do?

You must join hands with others. Once a difficult if not impossible task, now with an interactive internet it's very possible indeed. It will require dedication such as was put forward by the Coalition but it can be done. Proposed environmental rape must be met not only by people who live nearby but from every nook and cranny of the province.

It's either strength through unity or victims of the government's clever use of divide and conquer. That's the issue.

The First Thing We Do,
Let's Kill All the Lawyers

—Shakespeare, *Henry VI*

When there are too many policemen, there can be no liberty.
When there are too many soldiers, there can be no peace.
When there are too many lawyers, there can be no justice.
—Lin Yutang (1895–1976),
Chinese-American writer, translator and editor

B ack in February 2007 I read Jacqueline Windh's article
"Survivors Wait While Lawyers Squabble" in www.thetyee.ca
with many and mixed emotions. She was describing a series of hearings to determine how much each Native person should get from the damages the government promised to pay victims of sexual abuse in residential schools. I was ashamed of the way the Natives in the legal process Ms. Windh reported on were treated by the lawyers and the process in general, I felt shame at the delays which cost the victims so much distress and money, I felt shame that lawyers were taking a "cut" when liability wasn't in question, and mostly, I suppose, I felt ashamed of the profession I used to practise.

The hearings were to determine which of three categories of damages each individual was entitled to. This meant that people who are now elderly must tell all about what happened to them sixty or seventy years ago. This is not only a daunting task but it amounts, as we will see, to a search for evidence that the victim has suppressed and wants to keep that way—and forces the victim to relive his agony.

In Windh's article, Matthew Williams, a member of the Tla-o-qui-aht First Nation, sets the stage:

> Let me tell you what it's like at a hearing. I'm in a room, and there's my lawyer in front of me, an adjudicator to my right, two women from the government, and then one or two Native counsellors at my side, who I've never met before and who are usually *women*. Each time, I'm telling this to four different *women* [emphasis added] that I've never seen before and to an adjudicator who I've never seen before, trying to tell them about things that happened to me way back in 1951.
>
> They ask me, "What did it feel like when the priest stuck his penis up your ass for the first time? Did it hurt? Did it bleed? What did it feel like, having him breathing down your neck?" I was eight years old.

Who the hell would ask such a question? What client would permit his lawyer to act that way? The answer is that the lawyer is well trained by the system for the task of being a vicious cur for the federal government.

Since I left practice in December 1975, the demand for lawyers has increased exponentially (I don't think that was the result of my leaving!) and the cost of doing business has increased accordingly. According to the BC Law Society about 10,100 lawyers practice in British Columbia for a population of 4 million; until a short time ago there were only 8,000 lawyers in all of Japan for a population of 125 million. (That's changing, of course, as Japan rushes to join the US and Canada as one of the most litigious nations in the world.) The United States has a million lawyers for about 300 million people. While these are approximate numbers, they are close enough to tell us that our society supports a hell of a lot of lawyers.

According to *BC Work Futures*:

> In 2000, the average annual earnings for all individuals in this occupational group [the legal profession] were $99,200. The majority (76%) worked full-time for the full year, compared to 43% in the general workforce, and they received an average of $107,900 in earnings, which is more than double that of the average full-time full-year worker ($44,200). The number of those employed in this occupation rose from 6,180 in 1990 to 10,100 in 2001. About two years after graduation, university graduates starting out in this profession reported an average annual income of about $74,300.

I know that old when-I-was-a-boy stuff is hard to take, but I can tell you that in the '60s and '70s you made nowhere near the then-equivalent of $75,000 after two years, the reason being that, apart from the partners' frugality, there wasn't the amount of business there is today. But you can't blame young people for flocking to law schools when there's so much loot to divide. The cause and the cure rests with the public, so the question becomes: How do we reduce the supply of lawyers by reducing the demand for them? And the answer is simple: To reduce the number of players, you have to reduce and often eliminate the playing fields.

Some things have been done in that direction, such as increasing the jurisdiction of Small Claims Court to $25,000. But they should add a zero to that figure and hear all personal injury claims in that most efficient system. I suppose you should have a "however clause" if a judge decides the case should be held in Supreme Court, but such cases should be few in number. And Supreme Court Rules should be laid to rest and everyone start again. The opportunities these rules provide for lawyers to run up the bill are unbelievable, and they do so much of this legal featherbedding that they no longer realize that's what they're doing! They think that adjournment after adjournment to accommodate their schedules or that of the judge is beneficial to the client who must pay for all the applications to the judge for a postponement.

I remember when in practice one could make an application for a creditor, such as a bank, for "summary judgment" (Order XIV), meaning instant judgment. The onus was on the defendant to show why judgment ought to be against him. That old Order XIV undoubtedly still lives. The rule was designed for cases where it is simply money owed and there is no apparent defence. I once told a client that I could delay his case a year by making stalling applications to a judge in chambers, and I did! If I were still at the bar, I might be disbarred for admitting this but I'm not, and the practice was and is widespread. Why, just the possibilities for adjournment and other contentious and fee-producing delays prior to going to trial are enough to make it unprofitable for lawyers to get on with the actual trial too quickly or, perish the thought, settle out of court.

But something else has happened. Lawyers have drifted into a lot of areas that not only don't need them but suffer for their presence. I often used to ask, only partly tongue-in-cheek, why the hell I was an underpaid talk-show host when I could hang up my shingle again and get into the huge and flourishing Aboriginal claims feast of ever-fattening fees. And this, in my roundabout way, gets us back to Jacqueline Windh's story. Mr. Williams, who mentions having a lawyer in attendance at the hearing, could expect to pay him up to 40 percent of his award in legal fees. This is madness—and it is unconscionable. There is no question of liability, just a matter of deciding what category of compensation each claimant fits into, and that is determined by the claimant himself remembering and recounting enormous pain. Again I refer back to Small Claims Court and suggest that any of those judges—including retired Judge Alfred Scow, an aboriginal who has made an outstanding contribution to his people as well as to the public at large—could handle these matters quickly and fairly.

There is, of course, a place for questioning all claimants in any contentious matter. That, however, doesn't mean that claimants dealing with matters that occurred in their childhood should be treated by the system as if they are claiming in a bogus "whiplash" case. If, in these tragic cases of abuse of children taken from their culture by force and subjected to unspeakable acts fifty years ago, it should happen that one or two are, compared to the others, "overcompensated" (how you would define that I don't know), then so what? It can't possibly be worse than the moneys paid by ICBC out of our premium dollars to undeserving claimants every day of the year.

Most of all, though, there is no place for questions like, "What did it feel like when the priest stuck his penis up your ass for the first time? Did it hurt? Did it bleed? What did it feel like, having him breathing down your neck?" Any system that permits that sort of legal brutality needs instant overhaul.

Politics in Paradise

When I say that politics in BC is different than in other parts of Canada, those who live outside this province will laughingly agree that we're pretty goofy! In fact, we're not really that goofy if you understand what makes us tick. As I've noted elsewhere, if a prime minister were to come to BC to offer his support to a provincial party, it would sound the death knell for that party. In the last provincial election I advised the NDP that if they wanted to win they should find a way to get Jean Chrétien and Sheila Copps to come here and campaign for the Liberals.

From the day it came into Confederation in 1871, BC has had a hearty suspicion-unto-distaste for Ottawa. Even when the Ottawa and BC governments were of the same party, sparks flew. One of our Liberal leaders in the forties, Duff Pattullo, had huge battles with Mackenzie King's Liberal government. In 1952 W.A.C. Bennett co-opted a rather strange group called the Social Credit League and ran with it for twenty years. Mr. Bennett hadn't the faintest idea what Social Credit meant and couldn't have cared less; all that mattered was that it was a "BC-only" party. He ran a (mostly) free enterprise government that had absolutely no ties to any national party. (There was a period when Bennett held hands with the National Social Credit Party, but there never was the slightest possibility that the National Party would come to power.) When then Prime Minister Lester Pearson came to BC in 1964 to sign the Columbia River Treaty, he said, "I am the prime minister of Canada but Bennett is boss of all he surveys." When Bennett's creaking, aged government lost to the NDP in 1972, his son stepped in and reformed the Social Credit party and openly (and successfully) incorporated federal Liberals and Tories into what was called, pointedly, *the British Columbia Social Credit Party*. Again we had a provincial party that owed nothing to any national party.

When the NDP came in again, any ties they had with their federal wing were irrelevant since the federal NDP weren't in power or anywhere close to it.

The "BC only" party system reared its head again in 1996 when Gordon Campbell's Liberals blew an election to the NDP. This happened because neither the Social Credit Party nor the Reform Party would support them. After the election Campbell did what he should have done before—made it plain that the Liberal flag was one of convenience only, that his Liberals had no ties with any federal party and his party was really the Socreds again in thin disguise. Though Campbell has taken his party considerably to the right, he has the centre pretty well under control, and he has maintained the appearance of being a BC-firster, a prerequisite to victory on this side of the mountains.

Amazing Coincidences

I remember my Gram, Jane Macdonald from Cape Breton Island, telling me when I was a lad that Nova Scotian politics were full of amazing coincidences. For example, if a government was thrown out, the contractors building the roads would, by an amazing coincidence, find themselves replaced by the "other guys," usually the following morning. I must tell you that we're no slouches in that department in British Columbia; our politics is chock-a-block full of amazing coincidences.

Take John Duncan, the former member of parliament for Vancouver Island North. He was defeated in the 2006 federal election, as was the Liberal MLA for the area in the previous provincial election, on one issue: The farming of Atlantic salmon that is so prevalent in his former riding. At one time this seat had been safe for Duncan, but he got whupped because his constituents in the main could see how fish farms were raising havoc with wild salmon. So what happened when Prime Minister Harper decided that his Newfie minister of Fisheries needed some assistance with West Coast fishery matters? Who was the best man in the land for the job? By an amazing coincidence it happened to be none other than Mr. Duncan who now, having been thrown out of office for supporting Atlantic-salmon cages, was advising the minister of Fisheries and Oceans on the subject of fish farms.

In 2010 we will have, of course, the Winter Olympics. In order to get this, we had to promise a good highway to Whistler. One option, the cheaper one, was to put a road up Indian Arm to hook up to the old road. The other option was to widen the Sea-to-Sky Highway, thus creating all sorts of development opportunities. Gordon Campbell is a land developer by trade. It is his fellow developers who keep his election pots full. So by another amazing coincidence the more expensive Sea-to-Sky option with lots of developable land along the way was selected.

Then there was the fuss about the RAV (Richmond-Airport-Vancouver) line, now patriotically called the Canada Line so that, some cynics would say, people wouldn't remember they were one and the same project. The RAV line was so contentious, so unpopular with many member municipalities in the Greater Vancouver Regional District (GVRD) that the name had to be changed for the sake of keeping bad words in political conversations to a minimum. There was, you see, a perfectly good right-of-way along the old interurban lines that, complete with tracks, was there for the asking. The trouble was that many good BC Liberals (if that's not an oxymoron) had expensive homes along Arbutus Street beside the interurban tracks.

The Liberals, especially Stephen Owen, MP for Vancouver Quadra, didn't want that interurban line to be gussied up, even if the price was a fraction of what it would cost to build the RAV line. Then to the surprise of all, then-Mayor Larry Campbell, always assumed to be of the NDP persuasion, threw his considerable weight behind the RAV line. It was tough work. The GVRD and other political bodies kept holding votes that, alas for Larry, were opposed to the RAV. But Larry is a fighter and by arm wrestling and using all the political clout at his disposal to get approval, he succeeded. Then by another one of those amazing coincidences, the ink was hardly dry on the approval when His Worship quite suddenly accepted the Liberal government's offer of a senatorship.

Can Nova Scotia beat that for amazing coincidences?

Politics, 21st-Century Style

Never in my memory have political leaders been held in such low esteem—the polls don't show that?—and this is because there are no decent choices and comparisons must be made amongst those in power or trying to be. Smaller parties and independents have no chance of electing anyone.

In January 2003 Premier Gordon Campbell was arrested for drunk driving and had his prison photograph on the front pages of Canadian newspapers, making a fool of himself in the process and embarrassing the people of the entire province. Then, sitting in judgment of his own conduct, Mr. Campbell decided there was no political forfeit to pay. Clearly he was not to be judged by the standards he demanded of NDP cabinet ministers when he was in opposition. (His snivelling, cowardly excuse that he was on private time is nothing short of idiotic. Would it be acceptable if he robbed a bank, provided it didn't happen in BC and was done on his own time? Or is it only in Hawaii that he could steal and stay in cabinet?) Campbell excused himself by saying that he was re-elected, which is such a monstrous non sequitur that, even coming from him, it surprised me.

In February 2007, BC Mining Minister Bill Bennett (not the real one but the MLA for Kootenay East) sent a very rude email to a constituent. In this letter Mr. Bennett, amongst other things, said, "I am not about to take that kind of bullshit from someone who, for all I know, is up here as an American spy who is actually interested in helping the US create a park in the Flathead," the Flathead being in Mr. Bennett's riding. He wants mines there whereas the object of his disaffection wants a park. Bennett was a damned fool, but since when did that disqualify one from cabinet? Indeed, looking at how this and previous cabinets behave, one might have thought that being a "damned fool" was a condition precedent to being appointed (excepting the ones I was in, of course!).

Clearly Mr. Bennett did not appreciate how emails spread and how nearly all documents in government get spread about. (I remember the "real" Bill Bennett telling a cabinet of which I was a member, "Mark your documents 'SUPER CONFIDENTIAL' to ensure their widest possible circulation.") The remedy for this sort of offence is surely not resignation but an apology.

Many years ago when I represented Kamloops in the legislature and was a cabinet minister, I was faced with a Dr. Bob Woollard in Clearwater in my riding, who was leading a group opposed to uranium mining. I publicly called him as "red as baboon's ass" and used other similar pleasantries and I had a very angry citizenry to deal with. Determining that Dr. Woollard was more popular in Clearwater than I was, I convened a public meeting—they came from far and wide— and I apologized without reservation to the good doctor. After I had apologized, I stood there and took a hell of a lot of shit. I knew that my problem wasn't with Mr. Bennett (the real one) but with my constituents. I carried Clearwater handily in the next election in 1979. (Incidentally, Dr. Woollard and I met later and there were laughs and no hard feelings.)

Bill (not the real one) Bennett was forced to resign by the same Premier Gordon Campbell who was nailed for drunk driving and thus disgraced his office, the legislature and his province. This is the same Gordon Campbell who denied knowing Doug Walls, the man who was given $65 million of public funds to control while he was under investigation by special Crown counsel and the RCMP for fraud and forgery. (He later pled guilty to one charge and virtually got away scot-free.) In response to a series of ongoing questions Mr. Campbell denied knowing the man, said that just because Wall's wife was his wife's cousin meant nothing because his wife had lots of cousins. Then he admitted having met the man, then admitted that he had stayed with Mr. Walls in Prince George, and he finally admitted that he knew Walls well enough to go all the way to Prince George to lease a car from Mr. Wall's car dealership. And this man dared sit in judgment of Mr. Bennett. We all do wrong but the obvious rule is that unless you're Gordon Campbell you accept your medicine.

It's more than hypocrisy. The Campbell government has no moral compass. It can't possibly have one if the premier himself doesn't have one.

More Power to the People
Through Their MLAs

I was asked by a group of what you might call community agitators to tell them how they could get their environmental concerns listened to by the provincial government. They had tried their MLA with no success and wondered if they should attempt to meet with cabinet. These weren't naïve people. In fact, they were all successful in their lives.

I had to tell them how I, at forty-four years and a lawyer, became an MLA, which I assumed meant that I along with all other MLAs of all political stripes would sit down together and try to come up with legislation and policy for the general good of the province. I found out very quickly that nothing approaching that was going to happen. I was in the government caucus and the cabinet and immediately found that the cabinet (and because he appoints them, the premier) was the bullet-proof fount of all power. Indeed, the premier was the boss, period. I was part of a four-year dictatorship where party discipline was ironclad. (I didn't squawk. I took my cabinet seat without a murmur.)

The gulf between cabinet and the backbench is enormous. It's true that caucus members can raise hell in the caucus room, but they seldom do so for the very good reason that they want to join cabinet or at least become a parliamentary secretary or other position that brings more money and a title and that won't be easy if they don't seem to always be 100 percent for the team! When a minister brings his bill to caucus, members listen patiently, ask questions, make notes and that's where it ends. It's all over and not a damned thing has happened. Nor will it happen unless the premier wants it to. The bill is tabled in the House and passed by MLAs whether they understand it or like it.

So what is the citizen to do?

If your MLA is on the government side, you can join the party and try to bring your constituency organization's problem to your MLA. This is a waste of time and effort since, even if you were successful, your MLA would be unlikely to be able to do much about it unless he/she were in cabinet and even then it would need the premier's support. The other way is to contact the opposition MLA who is the critic for the area you're concerned about. He/she can at least make a noise where the government MLA cannot, but all you get is someone who might vocalize on the subject, ask questions in Question Period and the like—if his/her leader approves. It may come to pass that your opposition MLA becomes the government some day and will be able to change the law for you. But don't hold your breath for that to happen because now he's a backbench government MLA who, not in cabinet, is expected to do as he is told if he wants to be a minister some day.

This is, of course, why there are protest groups and why elderly grandmothers go to jail for contempt of a court orders. There are no meaningful environmental hearing proceedings, simply "information meetings" where you can ask questions, the answers to which are invariably guarded mumbo-jumbo. Even where there is a so-called hearing, the man making the decision works for the government. Worst of all, whatever hearings there are and whatever consultation happens always take place *after* the decision has been made.

The "democracy deficit," made so much of before the last federal election, equally applies to our legislature. Neither federal nor BC leaders have done a damned thing about it and won't, and they'll do nothing about the inability of ordinary citizens to have any say in policy. Premiers and prime ministers—and indeed cabinet ministers—like things the way they are and see no need for any but the most superficial of changes. This is the strongest of many strong arguments in favour of changing our manner of voting to the Single Transferable Vote system.

And we as a country have the nerve to tell other countries to get rid of their governments and do it our way!

Lady or Leader?

You have to wonder about BC NDP leader Carole James. Does she have the necessary royal jelly to become premier after the next election? Because if she doesn't, she won't be around for the one after that.

Ms. James is a very nice, decent human being. I like her very much—for whatever that might add to this discourse. But it looks a lot like she is too nice for the job. Robert Stanfield was too nice for the job and never became prime minister. Lester Pearson, another gentleman through and through, could never win a majority. John Turner and Joe Clark were nice guys and Kim Campbell a swell lady, but all were mere blips on the radar screen. Mike Harcourt is an obvious example of how a nice guy just can't stomach the stench of raw politics, which is a blood sport, and all the bleating about what it *should* be is wasted. It's a tough game if you're planning to win. You must be tough on your caucus, tough on your cabinet and tough on yourself.

It's here that many readers/listeners and I part company. Success in BC politics doesn't require nice people; indeed, it requires people with the ability, if not the desire, to attack the "other guys." One would have thought that the NDP had learned that lesson when former leader Bob Skelly, the nicest of the nice, got murdered in his only election as leader. He was too nice to be the leader of the opposition and too nice to make it to the premier's office.

Ms. James is under the handicap of opposing a government that in 2006 nearly didn't obey its own legislation and call a fall session, knowing that such arrogance wouldn't be punished. That would have eliminated question period where Ms. James could have turned her Rottweilers loose. But it also provided her with a golden opportunity to develop this obvious case of denial of democracy, and she should have crafted an appropriate slogan—"Bring back democracy—open the legislature!"—and barnstormed the province. When the government at the last minute called a short session to tidy up some stuff, it left the clear impression that this government could do as it liked without penalty.

Back in 1974 the NDP government passed a very sensible rule that the total time allotted for debating "estimates" be 135 hours. (The term "estimates" means that each cabinet minister must defend his spending, item by item, from opposition probing.) Bill Bennett's Socreds filibustered the debates so that when it came time for the finance minister to defend his estimates, time had run out. (I should add that the finance minister's estimates should take no more than a few minutes since he himself spends very little.) In any event, Bennett, every bit the thespian, stormed out of the legislature and went on a speechmaking spree around the province hollering, "Not a dime without debate!" The NDP, rising to the bait, fined Bennett for missing days in the House, thus making an impoverished hero out the multimillionaire premier-to-be on a phony-baloney issue. Bennett's actions were a big factor in the Socred victory in December 1975.

This is politics BC style; it's a blood sport. All Ms. James' political experience has been at the school board level where there is no official partisanship, where people don't lose their jobs if they disagree with the majority. Like most municipal leaders, Ms. James learned the wrong sort of politics to be trained for the BC legislature. Of course, the "higher purpose" people will gnash their teeth and prefer that Ms. James lead by showing manners. But as Leo Durocher, the famous baseball manager, once said, "Nice guys finish last."

It comes down to this: Does Carole James want to be a lady or a leader?

PART VI

Some People I Have Met

Some People I Have Met

The original *Vanity Fair* (1868–1914) was a British magazine renowned for its satirical cartoons, especially those by Leslie Ward, who signed himself Spy. I have collected Spy cartoons for years and have about a hundred. Most of mine are of British gentlemen about whom I know little if anything and are of no great value, but I do have the series of judges, which do have a little value. About twenty years ago I was in a bookstore in the famous Hay-on-Wye on the Welsh border, which is known as the used-book capital of the world, though Wigtown in Scotland might object. I chanced upon a Spy of Lord Randolph Churchill, father to Winston, and like an idiot, passed it up. My abiding interest was, of course, to obtain one of the two cartoons by Spy of Winston Churchill himself, which are quite expensive. I finally got one in May 2006 and it has pride of place in my Churchill collection.

I tell you all this because of Spy's shtick. He would try to catch his subjects when they didn't expect to be caught, so in fact he would have the equivalent of a snapshot. Over the years I've met many interesting people, on some of whom I have done my own verbal "Spy." The resulting sketches, I hasten to point out, are like Spy's cartoons: mere snapshots meant to convey an impression as many of the subjects deserve—indeed some have—biographies written about them. Most of my sketches are based on a short interview, though there are some you will recognize as being based on a longer exposure.

They are listed in no special order either by alphabet or importance. Having said that, I felt I wanted to start with the Churchill family and their associates.

Lady Soames (Mary Churchill) is the youngest of the Churchill family and bears a striking likeness to her mother, the famous "Clemmie." Now in her mid-eighties, she looks twenty years younger. She is upper class without being snooty—indeed, she refers to her life as being "upper class" without betraying any snobbery or boastfulness. During the London Blitz, she helped man an anti-aircraft gun in Hyde Park. She loved her parents very much and her first-class biography of her mother has been recently reissued. Quite a lady. I was fortunate to have interviewed her three times.

Grace Hamblin, Winston Churchill's principal stenographer for many years in peace and war, described how in the wee hours of the morning she would have to type the great man's words—no shorthand was allowed—and told of the stress, sometimes anger, often impatience with which she had to deal. On her death in 2002, Richard Langworth, a distinguished Churchillian and editor of the Churchill journal *Finest Hour*, had this to say about Miss Hamblin:

> Beloved by all Churchills, and the organizations that bear the name, Churchill Centre honorary member Grace Hamblin died at her home in Westerham, Kent on the morning of Tuesday, 15th October, aged 93. Grace Hamblin was the longest serving and most loyally devoted of Winston Churchill's inner circle, arriving at Chartwell in 1932 as an

assistant to then-principal private secretary Violet Pearman. She spent virtually her entire career as private secretary, first to Winston and from 1939 to Clementine Churchill. In 1966 she became the first Administrator of Chartwell, serving through 1973. In 1974 she was secretary to the Churchill Centenary Exhibition at Somerset House in London.

When I interviewed Grace Hamblin, it was like being at Chartwell, as I have been so many times, but with Churchill himself there. She spoke of the difficulties of working such terrible hours with such an unreasonable (by most standards) man. I asked her about his drinking and, while I don't recall her precise words, she made it clear that he was never the worse for wear.

Some time later a bit of research brought forth the following letter she wrote to the *British Medical Journal*, which had earlier printed an article bringing the issue of Churchill's drinking into play.

EDITOR: I have just read the outrageous attack on the late Sir Winston Churchill and am appalled that it should have appeared in what is generally regarded as a respectable publication. I joined Sir Winston's secretarial staff in 1932 and remained with his family until his death in 1965. In all those years, except for illness or holidays, I saw him almost daily and had a unique opportunity to watch his moods — sometimes sad, sometimes exuberant, but never the worse for drink.

Robertson [the author of the article] obviously bases his theory on scandalous hearsay. He would do well to study his subject a great deal more carefully before again writing such an ignorant and libelous attack—particularly on someone who is no longer here to defend himself.

Signed: Grace Hamblin

The *Journal's* editor promptly and profusely apologized.

Martin Gilbert, or more correctly Sir Martin, is probably the most productive top-notch non-fiction writer of all time with, at this writing, more than seventy-six non-fiction books to his credit. And unlike the stuff I put out, his is all deeply researched, serious stuff. He took over as Winston Churchill's official biographer after Randolph Churchill, Churchill's son and literary executor, died with two volumes completed, leaving Sir Martin to do the last six. However, he denies being the "official" biographer because the title is somewhat misleading. As he said in an interview with Brian Lamb on C-Span's "Book-Notes" in 1991, "I'm called the official biographer, though to the enormous credit of the Churchill family they've never asked to see a single word of what I was writing until the books were printed and bound and ready for sale to the public. They never asked me to delete a word or to skirt around a particular issue. So 'official' is a misnomer if it's thought to mean a censored or restricted biographer." Any who have read all eight of the Churchill volumes—and I certainly have—must marvel at the detail, especially in the last six books, as well as Sir Martin's assembly of ten huge companion volumes of Churchill documents.

I would say that his biography of the great Churchill is the achievement of a lifetime, but he is also the author of twin histories of the first and second world wars, the comprehensive *Israel: A History*, and a three-volume work, *A History of the Twentieth Century*. His book *The Holocaust: The Jewish Tragedy* is the definitive work on the subject. And I am now reading his book of letters to a Jewish lady in India that outlines the history of the Jews back to Adam and Eve.

When I interviewed him, I found Sir Martin to be concise and rather humourless, but I suppose after a writer of his attainments gets the same questions about Churchill thrown at him ad nauseum it's hard to be funny. However, through the *gravitas* the interviewer detects a man with the same capacity for work as his famous subject with, dare I say it, more thorough research. Mind you, Sir Martin has not been called upon to run too many wars! If nothing else, you should "google"

Sir Martin's bibliography and you will, like all who read it, be staggered by the output of this man who is not yet seventy.

I can't leave off the Churchills without mentioning **Mrs. Broome** whose first name I have, sadly, forgotten. In 1993 I led a tour of Britain and we were scheduled to be at Chartwell at four p.m. Unhappily, two of my crew got lost in Canterbury and we were obviously going to miss our appointment. The tour guide wrung his hands, not knowing what to do. "Is that not a phone there on the dash?" I asked. Indeed, it was. So I looked at our itinerary, found the number for Chartwell, phoned it and got Mrs. Broome, the lady in charge. I explained what had happened and how we had a busload of Canadian Churchill fans on board.

"Not to worry," said Mrs. Broome. "Get here as quickly as you can and we'll stay open for you." We did and she did—for a full hour.

Premier Gordon Campbell is an interesting study. He is a good conversationalist and witty. Publicly he's a tyrant. During the battle over the Kemano Completion Project (KCP) in 1993, as leader of the opposition, Campbell visited my studio and reviewed the mountains of evidence we had. He came out against KCP, and his opposition made Premier Mike Harcourt's decision to tube the project considerably easier. Then, after he became premier, over lunch with me he asked me to give him more information on Atlantic salmon fish farms, information I had collected while conducting a vigorous campaign against them. He told me that during the KCP fight he had seen a billboard showing migrating sockeye salmon and that he had vowed that his children and grandchildren would be able to see this sight. Yet, from that moment on, he fought as hard as he could *for* fish farms. At his request I sent a paper I had prepared that included the opinions of the world's main scientists working in this area and I didn't even get a reply. I should have known better but I honestly believed that he would be a political environmentalist. I've been told that he has no desire to admit that Rafe Mair might be right.

Premier Campbell did what he said he would do on the electoral reform issue: He set up a citizens' assembly and, when a change was recommended, put the proposed change to a referendum. However, this evidence that Campbell is a democrat is offset by the iron-fisted way he runs government and what can only be assumed is deliberate indifference to environmental issues.

Unless there is a sea change in current BC politics, Gordon Campbell should win handily in 2009 because he is tough and disciplined and for that reason will be hard to beat. The political path of politics is strewn with the corpses of "nice" politicians who have brought good manners and a sunny disposition to the legislature or parliament because the public prefers a tough and hard-nosed leader to one who wishes to be cooperative and soft-spoken.

Jimmy Carter came to be interviewed by me for a very unusual reason—he had written a neat little book on fly-fishing. The ex-president had in fairly recent times been bitten by the fly-fishing bug and his experiences brought out the author in him. I don't remember much about the interview except when, once again disobeying orders, I asked him how he felt when the American hostages in Iran were released the day Ronald Reagan replaced him in the White House. Instead of walking away from the question, he gave a detailed, well-thought-out and gracious answer. I admire Jimmy Carter and thought he was a better president than the generally Republican media did, and I suspect that my audience came away from the interview thinking, as I did, that we had listened to a class act.

Carl Brewer was a fine if not great hockey player and a Hall of Famer; **Susan Foster** was his partner and one very gutsy lady. The owners of the National Hockey League had stolen huge sums of money from the players' pension fund that had been set up in the '40s to take care of players, many of whom had been pressured into forfeiting higher education to play hockey. Moreover, they had played when salaries were infinitesimal and if injuries shortened or ended a career—too bad. What the owners had done was simple theft. They took the interest the pension plan earned and pocketed it. When the players challenged this fraud, the owners decided to "money whip" them with high-powered lawyers and endless court procedures that eventually went to the Supreme Court of Canada in 1994. Carl Brewer and his fighting consort took on the owners without money, courage being the best they could bring to the fight. The media, with but one or two exceptions—Bruce Dowbiggin being the lonely Canadian exception and, may I immodestly say, joined by Rafe Mair—either pretended the issue wasn't there or openly supported crooks like Alan Eagleson who represented about four hundred players and stole from many of them, including Bobby Orr. Though the players won in the Supreme Court of Canada, the owners still dragged their heels by saying that computing the damages was too complicated. It wasn't too complicated to steal, just too complicated to make amends.

Because I had joined the fight in Vancouver, I met with and had numerous phone conferences with Carl and Susan during which I joked with Brewer that I was even prepared to forgive him for being a Maple Leaf. Tragically, he died before he got much benefit from the wars he had led, but he left a legacy of enormous courage, courage which might not have been there had he not had the partner he did. Carl Brewer and Susan Foster—true Canadian heroes.

Jimmy Pattison. I hold the distinction of having been fired twice by Vancouver billionaire Jimmy Pattison. It was said—and Jimmy later told me it was true—that when he first ran a car business, at the end of the month he would fire the salesman who had the fewest sales. He said that, if there were extenuating circumstances like illness or a death in the family, he took that into account and did nothing. "But

Rafe," he told me, "I did the man no favour keeping him on if he was no good."

Over the years I got to know Jimmy a bit better as we had come to like one another. I had lunch with him occasionally and from time to time I was also invited out for a cruise on his immense yacht, the *Nova Spirit*. An evening on Jimmy's yacht is interesting because he usually puts people together with a plan obviously in mind. Often times I found myself on board with people I didn't like and who didn't like me. As you might suspect, he enjoyed seeing what would happen. We were also all expected to say a few words on who we were and what we did—we sang for our supper, so to speak. I was, I think, sort of blacklisted for a while because I turned down an invitation that didn't include my wife. Maybe I wasn't persona non grata but that's the way it seemed.

Stephen Harper is not easy to love. On more than one occasion he stood me up for an appearance on my show. On at least one occasion he phoned in five minutes after his agreed time and I wouldn't put him on because I had the full board of callers I had asked for because we had lost our guest. Mr. Harper is dogmatic, although he will change his mind if the voter heat gets too much, such as when he wouldn't allow the media to be present when the bodies of Canada's Afghanistan war casualties were brought home. He also changed his mind on the Mulroney/bags of money probe when it got through to him that he was going to suffer politically if he didn't announce one.

Mr. Harper has an attitude towards Quebec that is dangerous because, like Brian Mulroney, he offers not just money as a bribe but, by designating them a "nation," constitutional power as well. But the key to his success will be helping Ontario as the price of oil goes up without alienating his core support in Alberta and British Columbia.

The Prime Minister isn't a fun guy to be with and if he has a sense of humour it's been well disguised. Having said that, if Liberal leader Stéphane Dion doesn't come up a better platform than simply

"Throw out the Tories," federal politics may become like BC provincial politics. Mair's Axiom II is that you don't have to be a ten in politics—you can be a three if everyone else is a two. Harper is clearly a three in a sea of twos.

Jack Layton looks like the standard caricature of a used car salesman and sometimes acts like it as he smothers issues with nice-sounding but empty phrases. A very decent man, he is like both Paul Martin and Stephen Harper in at least one respect—if he has a sense of humour, he keeps it well hidden. He has accomplished one thing, though—without the numbers to back him up, he has convinced many people that he has the balance of power. The one who recognizes that he's peddling horse buns is the Prime Minister who knows it's the Bloc Québécois who have the hammer, and Mr. Harper has shown a remarkably sure touch—so far—with the Quebec electorate.

Jack Layton carries with him the sad but true fact that the NDP can never get elected in Canada. On that score he's in the same position every leader of the NDP/CCF has been in going back to J.S. Wordsworth, the only difference being that Mr. Layton talks a better game and tries to give the impression that there is a Camelot in sight instead of taking advantage of the Liberals' lack of leadership to be a better opposition. What the NDP needs now more than ever before is a much younger Dave Barrett with the discipline of an Ed Broadbent.

Roy Jenkins, Lord Jenkins of Hillhead, was often considered along with his early colleague, Hugh Gaitskill, the best prime minister Britain never had. More of an old-fashioned liberal than a socialist, as a reforming home secretary he helped get the sixties swinging by relaxing the laws relating to abortion, censorship, divorce and homosexuality. As chancellor of the exchequer he helped restore Labour's credibility after the devaluation crisis of 1967 which ironically cost him his seat in the next election. Although he served a second spell as home secretary when Labour returned to power in 1974, he left parliament two years later to become Britain's first president of the European Commission.

I found his lordship's views on politics fascinating for it was he, in a dramatic move in 1981, who led three colleagues—Bill Rodgers, Dr. David Owen and Shirley Williams—out of the Labour Party to form the Social Democrats, which later joined up with the Liberals to become the Liberal Democrats. Most observers, including me, feel that the success of "New Labour," as developed by John Smith, Neil Kinnock and Tony Blair, in drawing middle-of-the-road supporters into its fold had a lot to do with Jenkins and his colleagues showing them the way to do it as well as demonstrating that, if Labour didn't move to the centre, it would continue to lose.

After earning a life peerage, Jenkins became chancellor of Oxford University and wrote acclaimed biographies of political figures such as Truman, Gladstone and Churchill, and it was as Churchill's biographer that I interviewed him. He told me that he had been to Vancouver many times and it had always rained—as it did that day.

His biography of Churchill came after the one on Gladstone. It is an excellent book and it's interesting to note that His Lordship started the Churchill book convinced that Gladstone was the best man ever to live in #10 Downing Street in modern times. But he changed his mind to Churchill after his deep research into the lives and careers of both men.

The late Lord Jenkins' colleague, **Denis Healey**, was also an outstanding man, and I interviewed him on his autobiography, *Denis Healey: The Time of My Life*. To me he was interesting as a contrast with Tony Benn whom I also interviewed around the same time, Benn having moved left if anything since his youth while Healey seemed to have moved to about the same place Lord Jenkins was. I realize that these "right/left" distinctions can be misleading, but since the Second World War the Labour Party has had pretty obvious lines of demarcation as it moved from its traditional perch on the "left" towards New Labour under Tony Blair. But Healey's move to the right was more spectacular than that of other Social Democrats since he had been, in his Oxford days, an outspoken Communist.

The former **Lord Anthony Wedgwood Benn** was a fascinating interview when I met him at his house across from Holland Park. In November 1960 His Lordship's father had died, passing his peerage on to him and thus disqualifying him from sitting in the House of Commons. Even so, he fought to retain his seat in the by-election caused by his succession, and although he was disqualified from taking his seat, the people of Bristol South-East re-elected him. Again he was not permitted to take his seat.

On July 31, 1963, legislation was passed giving peers the right to renounce their peerages, which Benn promptly did to become plain and simple Tony Benn. In an act of generosity one would be surprised to see elsewhere, the man he had defeated for his seat when he was disqualified promptly resigned the seat, and after winning a by-election on August 20, Benn returned to the Commons.

When I went to Benn's home, his den looked a lot like my den—books and papers all over hell's half-acre! He was charming but unrelenting in his criticism of how he saw, at that time, the Labour Party moving right in order to become electable. He remains active and represents what is left of the "old" and doctrinaire socialists in the Labour Party.

Mike Harcourt is, to say the least, an interesting man. He is affable and fun to be with so it's easy to see how people elected him to lead and then were disappointed. Not a natural New Democrat, he was appalled when the scandal involving Dave Stupich and what became known as "Nanaimo-gate" finally broke its bounds. Though utterly uninvolved in the matter, Harcourt handled it badly and felt constrained to resign, which he did—leaving us to Glen Clark and the fast ferries fiasco.

Mike's great courage was demonstrated when he persevered after a nasty fall that could well have made him a paraplegic, and though he must now use a cane, he gets around very well indeed. As a guest on air, he was the best I ever saw at running out the clock, so when he came on my show during the Charlottetown Accord, I had my producers book him (he was BC premier at the time) for two hours because, while I knew he could tap dance for an hour, I didn't think he could go longer. I was right. In the second hour he got crucified by the callers.

He "wrote" a book that I haven't read because I refuse to read as-told-to books. I understand that there are lots of references to me in it, none flattering, but on the premise that all publicity is good publicity, I should thank him. In fact, in my books Mike Harcourt is a helluva good guy—just a lousy premier. (He is also a great collector of well-paid sinecures.)

Glen Clark is a man of ambition and a bright guy. His trouble was that he's not as bright as he thought he was. The "fast ferries fiasco" was his baby and he went ahead against all advice, some of which even came from friendly quarters. But his downfall over the gambling issue was just plain stupid and from the outset I asked, "How could any senior politician be so dumb?" When I was in charge of liquor under Bill Bennett, W.A.C. Bennett gave me great advice: "Rafe, don't ever meet with liquor people without someone with you." And he was dead right. Clark, by a having a friendly relationship with a man wanting a gambling licence, killed himself politically. It's too bad because, if he'd had good advice and had listened to it, he might still be premier. I thought the charges against him were ill-considered, and after the Crown had finished its case, I said, "It reminds me of that Peggy Lee favourite, 'Is That All There Is?'" That he landed a good job with

Jimmy Pattison and has done well since then doesn't surprise me.

Ujjal Dosanjh, who succeeded Glen Clark as premier—the first non-white in Canada to be a first minister—inherited an unholy mess. He had been attorney-general when it hit the fan for Premier Clark, and he regularly caught hell from me thereafter because, once he knew the premier was under investigation for a crime, he should have advised him that he had a duty to resign and that he, Dosanjh, would otherwise be forced to quit. There is considerable misunderstanding about this rule. If a minister of the Crown is under a cloud, it's not a matter of innocent until proved guilty; he *must* resign until the matter is resolved. While Dosanjh was indeed dealt a tough hand, he should have gone to the people right after he became leader. Not that he would have won, but he would have had enough members to make up a decent opposition. As is usually the case, the longer an unpopular government postpones going to the people, the worse it is likely to get.

Dosanjh, a man I very much like, became an asterisk in our list of premiers right alongside Rita Johnston. It was another case of "I should have gone sooner."

The late **Anita Roddick** was the founder of The Body Shop. She was funny but serious. She hated capitalism and capitalists, though she became one of the richest people in the world. She tried her best to give her money away but made it too fast. I found that Ms. Roddick oozed sex appeal, and one of my producers later commented that the lady had been "coming on to me," which flattered me to no end. Ms. Roddick's hatred of "the City," London's Wall Street, knew no bounds. She was passionate in her caring for animals and maintained that none of her products are tested first on animals, though there are some who say otherwise. A very interesting person indeed.

King Michael I of the Romanians, a great-great-grandson of Queen Victoria and a third cousin of Queen Elizabeth II, is one of the last two living heads of state from the World War II era. King Michael did well in the private sector, though my interview with him in 2003 dwelt mainly on the wartime years when his father with his mistress, Elena Magda Lupescu, a woman of Jewish descent, was forced to abdicate in Michael's favour. At the time I interviewed him, he and Queen Anna hoped to be called back to reign. But although he visited Romania and received a tumultuous reception, there was no throne offered. So there they were, a king and his consort, both of royal blood and regal bearing, accepting their lot but still in their minds ready to go back and do their duty for their country.

Lord Montague of Beaulieu, (pronounced Bewly) is the owner of not only one of the finest stately homes in Britain but also of the National Motor Museum. This museum has cars, cars, and more cars, plus hands-on exhibits, rides, a monorail, gardens, driving games, parklands, and the family home, Palace House, built around the gatehouse of a Cistercian Abbey and containing an exhibition about the monks as well as the to-be-expected souvenir shop. It's a full day's proposition to visit. (I had actually visited the museum before my interview with Lord Montague.) Like an oak from an acorn, the whole project began in the front hall of Palace House. A mere five veteran vehicles were put on show when the place was opened to visitors in 1952, a fitting tribute to Lord Montague's father who was well-known in his day for his enthusiastic support for early motoring. Since then, the collection has grown to over 300 vehicles of all types and added a vast selection of associated items. In fact, so large are the numbers now that, even with the large exhibition hall, it's possible to show only around 250 vehicles at any one time.

I found out after my interview with Lord Montague that there was more to the man than met the eye. In 1954 he had been imprisoned for twelve months for consensual homosexual offences along with journalist Peter Wildeblood and Michael Pitt-Rivers. Unlike the other defendants in the trial, Montague continued to protest his innocence. The trial was a consequence of concern in the early 1950s about the increasing incidence of homosexuality, although ironically the anti-homosexual backlash led to the Wolfenden Report, which recommended decriminalizing homosexuality.

I'm not sure how I would have handled this information if I had known (in my own defence I have to say that there was no internet with "Google" at hand in those days), but I think I would have asked him how it felt to be singled out for punishment while Noel Coward, Somerset Maugham, John Gielgud and Cecil Beaton, to name a few prominent gays, were not. In any event, I stuck with motor cars and missed a potential interview of great if perhaps salacious importance.

Prince Charles is a strange man as we all know from what we hear, but all I can say after meeting him twice, once at Government House in Victoria when he and his father visited and the second time at Highgrove in Gloucestershire when I was among perhaps thirty journalists from all over the world, is that he is a grandmaster at spouting the inane crap such people are known for. The only other thing I noticed was that he is always playing with his cufflinks. He sort of reminds me of Prince George of Denmark, the husband of England's Queen Anne whose uncle, Charles II, once said of him, "I've tried him drunk and I've tried him sober and there's nothing in him."

The foregoing is, of course, somewhat unfair. The social march the senior royals must do for their lifetime is inhuman. Charles has had a lot of very bad press while, in fact, he is owed a debt of considerable proportion for the work his charitable trust has done and for protecting Paternoster Square by St. Paul's from the ravages that developers and their architects proposed. We could do with him in BC to deal with Gordon Campbell and his developer friends. But I still wonder if it wouldn't be better to have buttoned cuffs, although I suppose that there are worse habits than playing with your cufflinks.

Prince Andrew is quite a different breed of a cat from his brother. I met him at another reception at Government House in Victoria and I actually managed to have a decent talk with His Royal Highness about fishing. "Fergie," his estranged wife, had made headlines by that time and I would have loved to chat with him a bit about toe-sucking but thought better of it.

While he was still president of Israel, **Chaim Herzog** came to Vancouver, and I met him on Jimmy Pattison's yacht on an evening supper cruise in his honour up the North Arm of Burrard Inlet. Instead of the usual procedure where Jimmy had all his guests give a bit of a talk, the floor was turned over to Mr. Herzog, and to say the least, his talk on the new world unfolding since the fall of the Iron Curtain was riveting. During the question period I asked him about the many former Soviet republics in Asia and the impact of them selling their natural resources on the world market. His view was that when these republics settled their political situations—which would take time—they would have a formidable effect, and he expressed deep concern about the economic and political ramifications of their production of oil and natural gas.

It was quite an evening, but I would have loved a private interview where we could get down to cases about Israel, Palestine and neighbouring countries, subjects that would have been rather out of place on this social occasion.

I first met **Ralph Nader** at a private dinner in Victoria in 1976 before he was to take the stage of the Royal Theatre for a speech about the terrible ways of the automobile industry. He was both fascinating and dull at the same time; fascinating because he had done so much in the automobile industry with his blockbuster book, *Unsafe At Any Speed*, dull because he tended to drone on interminably, especially when he had the stage of the theatre all to himself. I next met him in the run up to the 2004 US presidential election in which he was determined to run. I asked him the questions you would expect about splitting the vote (which he did) but essentially got nowhere. Again, fascinating but dull.

I had two non-interviews over the years, one of which I'm especially annoyed about. The first no-show was **Brian Mulroney** who was scheduled to do my entire program on the Friday before the vote on the Charlottetown Accord. By the time we were in the last week it was clear that the Accord was going to fail and the prime minister no doubt knew that he would get beaten up for nothing. It being 3rd and 10, Mulroney elected to punt and, as I had predicted to my audience all along, he was a "no-show." The other non-interview was the UN arms inspector in Iraq, **Scott Ritter**. Turning him down was a huge mistake for I simply swallowed the line that Ritter was, if not a "nutcase," too eccentric to be taken seriously. This was at a time I supported action in Iraq—not on the say-so of Bush, Rumsfeld or Cheney but because I thought Colin Powell and Tony Blair could be trusted. It was a horrible decision and I think about it a lot.

PART VII

In Memoriam

A Death Like Few Others

It was a dullish April morning and somehow my muses weren't working as I stared at the keyboard. Then I noticed the date: April 12, 2007, the sixty-second anniversary of the death of Franklin Delano Roosevelt. The only comparable public outpouring of grief for a politician that I can remember was when JFK was assassinated.

I was in school at the time of Roosevelt's death. Our homeroom master was a Mr. Heidt (called Horace by the kids after the popular leader of a dance band) who was, we all felt sure, utterly devoid of emotion. But he came into the room with tears freely flowing down his cheeks and told us of FDR's death from a massive stroke at Warm Springs, Georgia. Many of us cried, too. The headmaster, "Johnny" Harker, called for an instant "parade" of all students and he addressed them with tears running down his cheeks. Afterwards, we all went into chapel and sang "God Bless America" and "Oh God, Our Help in Ages Past," and whatever tears were left flowed in time to that lovely anthem.

Why this grief for an American and in a British-style school with British masters! I guess it was sort of a case of "you had to be there."

To begin with, Roosevelt was seen as Churchill's friend and that went a very long way with us. We knew about the war, Lend-Lease, and the massive US forces fighting in Europe and the South Pacific. Up until that point, no doubt, many Canadians were still angry that the US hadn't come in earlier, but Roosevelt was the man who got it done. What could we now expect from Harry Truman, a failed haberdasher who was slightly tainted by his association with "Boss" Prendergast in Kansas City? Would he carry on the fight? Would FDR's death change how the war was to be fought?

It was then a combination of shock, fear and admiration, if not love, that shook us. And everybody from that day who is still alive knows where he was and what he was doing the day Franklin Delano Roosevelt died.

The Horrible '60s

O n November 22, 1963, I was in my law office in downtown
Vancouver when I received a call from my wife: President
John Kennedy had been shot and it was not known if he would live.
I went immediately to the corner of Georgia and Granville where
there was a newsboy (that long ago!) and a moving sign on the side
of the Hotel Vancouver, which sadly changed from "Kennedy shot"
to "Kennedy assassinated." The feeling was indescribable. Most were
thunderstruck. Many cried. Some rejoiced (some Americans had a
party to celebrate) and others were indifferent.

It was part of a horrible decade that saw John F. Kennedy,
Malcolm X, Medgar Evers, Martin Luther King and Bobby Kennedy
murdered. It seemed as if it would never end. And it started another
era, that of an America split over Vietnam. While the American
involvement in Southeast Asia had started back in Eisenhower's
time, Lyndon Johnson inherited the mess and decided to see the war
through. Air Force General Curtis LeMay—who, as General "Buck"
Turgidson, is beautifully parodied by George C. Scott in the 1964
movie *Dr. Strangelove*—wanted to bomb the North Vietnamese back

into the Stone Age. The United States was, for the first time since the Civil War, divided on a war and looked as if it might implode.

We were in the midst of a huge social upheaval. Blacks were going to school with whites, and getting a black, James Meredith, enrolled at the University of Mississippi on October 1, 1962, brought death and destruction until the deed was done. Then George Wallace, the last of the redneck governors, was permanently crippled by an assassination attempt. It was the time of the Beatles, of bare-breasted waitresses, and a never-ending supply of LSD and pot.

The '60s, which really embraced the end of the '50s and up to about 1968, were exciting years but terrible ones. And three names stand out: John F. Kennedy, Robert F. Kennedy and Martin Luther King. Although the greatest shock came forty-three years ago when the young president in whom so much hope had been placed was taken from us, the most profound legacy is that of Mr. King. How can I make this claim? Because it did. His death marked the very bottom of the terrible race relations that had existed while at the same time it made the climb up and out of that apparent abyss possible. His message, "I have a dream," has taken his life and example down to today and it will live on. It was a dreadful decade but, happily, some of the light that shone then has stayed with us. The light that Martin Luther King shone will never be extinguished.

My own lasting memory of that decade is of taking on as a client the seventeen-year-old son of a golfing friend. He was charged with being in possession of some pot and I had to tell his dad and him that, because of a Court of Appeal ruling, the lad would get six months in jail! I remember standing beside him as he shook like a leaf. What an awful age we were going through! But what a great age to have ended on a farmer's field near Woodstock, New York, in a love-in of drug-soaked, ill-clad young men and women rolling around as they played or listened to the awful sounds they called music.

The '60s? Good riddance.

On Remembering Denny Boyd

I found myself unable, because of a previous unbreakable commitment, to attend the funeral in October 2006 of Denny Boyd, one of Canada's best columnists, though he wasn't perhaps known as such by people outside of BC because little done by us on the West Coast is seen elsewhere. I was not an old friend of Denny's. I first met him back in the '70s when I was the minister responsible for booze in this province and Denny, for journalistic reasons no doubt but as a major consumer, too, wanted to see what the "liquor czar" looked and sounded like.

In 1981 after Denny had lost yet another battle to John Barleycorn, *The Vancouver Sun* newspaper agreed to keep him on provided he joined AA and sort of confess his sins publicly. (Only a newspaper would demand that a guy getting "anonymous" help would have to self-flagellate in public!) Part of the latter exercise was appearing on my show, which was then on CJOR 600. He made a virtue out of necessity and told his story in a self-effacing, funny way, but not in the slightest obsequiously. Denny never touched another drop.

He was an excellent writer. He had catholic interests; he could write on fishing, music, current affairs and nothing very much and still keep your attention. He was the columnist's columnist. And he had a lovely way of disguising thoughts with subtle humour. I wasn't the only politician who read one of Denny's columns and said, "Gee, Denny was really kind to me," then reread it only to see that he had neatly and deliciously cut his subject into little bits.

A few years ago I was at the launching of his latest book, timed to coincide with his "retirement." I, among others, was asked to do a reading and say a couple of words. I remember saying—and meaning it, "Denny, all one can ever be is the best of his time – and you are definitely the best of yours." (This bun toss had some funny moments, such as when Jack Webster, perhaps a bit too far into the nectar of his ancestors, in the same speech told the same story, word for word, twice!)

Denny didn't quite retire; he spent his later years writing a weekly column in the *North Shore Outlook*, a David Black community paper published in North Vancouver, and I had the privilege of writing a column alongside his. When he was diagnosed with cancer of the bladder about a year before his death, he refused to undergo chemotherapy, saying that he had put enough poisons in his body as it was. He died as he lived, with class and courage.

He's missed by his family, of course. And he is very badly missed by a profession that needs all the good ones it can find and by the legions of people who read him. May you have peace, Denny, an eternity of peace. And so say all of us who were lucky enough to know you as well as read you.

The Death of a Great One

I t was in May or June of 1948 when I took my sweetheart, Heather, to the old Palomar Supper Club where the Burrard Building in downtown is now. We were going to see Frankie Laine at the kids' matinee.

Laine was really big in those days. Huge. The bobbysoxers, as young girls were called then, screamed and fainted just as they had done a few years earlier with Frank Sinatra (to whom Laine was related). Laine was terrific. He came out to "By the River Sainte Marie," gave us his big hits—"That's My Desire," Fats Waller's "Black and Blue," and my favourite, "Blue Turning Grey Over You." And many others. Heather and I had had our picture taken by the street photographer who then plied his trade on Granville Street and Frankie signed it: "To Heather and Rafe, Thanks, Frankie Laine." It was a big thrill for a sixteen- and fifteen-year-old. I must ask Heather if she still has that picture!

Laine's orchestra leader was pianist Carl Fischer and together they made great music until Fischer suddenly died. Laine then moved over to Columbia and into the clutches of Mitch Miller and, although they made some hits, they were crap like "Mule Train,"

"The Cry of the Wild Goose" and "Jezebel." Many of his fans didn't realize that the jazzmen regarded him as one of them until crap like the "Wild Goose" came along, and, in fact, you can get a marvelous CD of Laine singing with Buck Clayton and his orchestra which will amply prove that point.

In the late '60s my wife Eve and I and another couple went down to the Cave Supper Club on Hornby to see Frankie Laine, and mercifully he laid off most of the cowboy junk, sang old songs and some new love songs he'd just released which, while not runaway hits, sold well. After the second show I told the group I would go up to the dressing room and get autographs. I told Mr. Laine what a fan I was and how I used to go to Seattle to get his stuff on the Atlas Label, not available here. I told him how "Someday, Sweetheart," "Coquette" and "You Can Depend on Me" were my favourites but were only on the Atlas label.

He expressed great surprise. "You mean you went all the way to Seattle just to get my Atlas stuff?" Then he asked, "What are you and your wife going to do now?"

I told him we would be heading home, but he wouldn't hear of it and insisted on taking us to a very late dinner at a wonderful Italian restaurant across the street. (Unfortunately, I've forgotten its name but it's long gone.) We finally got home about four a.m., and then the next afternoon, at his request, I went to his room at the Georgia Hotel and he showed me some new stuff he was working on.

Five years ago, I interviewed Frankie Laine for my show on CKNW. He professed to remember me well and we had a great interview. He was in good health and still doing some performances.

On February 6, 2007, we learned he had died at ninety-three. Something inside me and many others of my vintage died, too, for Frankie Laine had given us unforgettable memories of when we were young, untroubled and in love. I hope that Frankie Laine will now, as he sang in his big hit "That Lucky Old Sun," "roll around heaven all day."

PART VIII

The Sporting Life

I Hate the Maple Leafs
More Than I Hate the Yankees

O kay, fellow Toronto Maple Leaf haters (and Blue Jay and Argo haters while we're at it), it's time to show some mercy. I daresay I go back further in my Leaf hating than 99 percent of you and maybe age brings mercy, but I'm beginning to feel a little sorry for the phuquers . . . oops, I mean fans.

I started back in the War—no, not the First World War, Number Two, dammit—when it was entirely on radio, and the CBC determined that all we could safely hear were the games from Maple Leaf Gardens, the home of Conn Smythe and real Canadian heroes, and that those slackers and yellow bellies in Montreal must be ignored as a matter of the "war effort." Foster Hewitt, who made Bob Cole and Harry Neale sound even-handed, was the most biased announcer I've ever heard. According to him, the hated Montreal Canadiens, my beloved Habs, had a yellow streak down their back when they played real CANADIAN boys. It was awful.

The between-periods chat by the "Hot Stove" made it clear that the only reason other teams were in the league was to provide the Leafs (the plural of "leaf" is "leaves" everywhere else in the world) a modicum of competition on their annual march to the Stanley Cup. The "three stars" were often a load of laughs. If Montreal beat the Leafs 8–2, the first star would be the Montreal goalie Bill Durnan, the suggestion being that it would have been 9–8 for the Leafs had he not played so brilliantly.

I had some bad times as the world's most devoted Canadiens fan. The year 1967 comes to mind when I was in Maple Leaf Gardens to see the Leafs beat the Habs 3–1 (last goal on an empty net) for the Cup. Such was my despair that, as I rode the subway home to where I was staying, I was sure everyone was staring at me. Mostly, though, it was great—especially in 1960 when Montreal won the Cup in eight straight, the last four against the Leafs. The last game was 4–0 Habs with Rocket Richard scoring the fourth goal, his last in the NHL.

But Jeez, folks, it's been forty-one years—forty-one!—since those pricks have been in the finals (Vancouver has been there twice since then), and most of the fans have never even heard of Syl Apps, Ted Kennedy or Turk Broda. Foster Hewitt is a name they might recall their grandparents mentioning. They're decent people, they deserve better. Let's all pull for the Leaves this year and get them into the playoffs and help them win the Cup! It's the decent thing to do, isn't it? On the other hand . . . fuck 'em!

I Went to the Fights
and a Hockey Game Broke Out

Early in 2007 the *Vancouver Province* set out to decide who was the best hockey fighter of all time. They did it like a tennis draw, matching pairs and making up winners until there were two left. Even if they could have told who would have beaten whom—a dubious assumption indeed—this method has all the frailties of match play in golf that never tells you with any accuracy who was best in the tournament, just who never lost a match, which is quite a different thing. Now if the "seed" had been different, the ultimate winner might have lost in the first round. So even if the *Province* could accurately predict the outcome of each "fight," if the draw had been different, it probably would have produced a different winner. But why in the first place would a paper that passes itself off as a community-oriented journal support fights in hockey? What does that say to kids?

One night when I was having dinner at the Red Lion, our favourite restaurant, there being no hockey game on, TSN had elected to spend about an hour featuring hockey fights! Not first-class goals or even miraculous saves, but *fights*. It reminds one of the old saw: "I went to the fights and a hockey game broke out."

I was at my daughter's house one night for dinner and, it being a hockey house, I accidentally saw part of a game. I saw quickly why I don't watch hockey anymore—nowadays I haven't a clue who's where or why. It was between periods when I joined the game so I had the dubious privilege of seeing Don Cherry. That was enough. I know Cherry is colourful and should not be taken too seriously, but I draw a straight line from him to a horrible fight a few days earlier when a Maple Leaf player was beaten, fell head first on the ice and was concussed. The man who did the damage was quoted as saying, "That's hockey!" And that's Don Cherry's and the NHL's attitude, and I don't like it.

The excuse offered by the media is that hockey is a fast, hard-hitting game and the boys have to let off steam! This is crap. Basketball, with no padding, is a fast and relatively hard-hitting game and fights are simply not tolerated. Nor are they tolerated in rugby, football or soccer. Moreover, you don't expect to see Vijay Singh stick a putter up Tiger Woods' ass when he's about to sink the winning putt! Silly argument? Not so. Classy sports make competitors play by rules. This nonsense about young full-blooded examples of Canadian youth showing off Canadian manliness is a terrible indictment of us and what was once our game.

Why is fighting encouraged in hockey? The answer is that the owners know the fans love fights and, if it reduces the stature of hockey from being a major sport to something only marginally better than a roller derby, who cares? The fans, paying unbelievable money for the privilege, flock in to see it, and that's the only thing that matters. We are a violent people and part of a violent species of animal. The *Vancouver Province* didn't do its series without knowing what fan reaction would be nor did the TV station run all those fights just for the hell of it. When the fans sit on their hands instead of cheering, when they walk out rather than asking for more, then and only then will the fights stop.

Whenever hockey is seriously discussed, nostalgia brings back the famous 3–3 tie between the Montreal Canadiens and the Red Army team on December 31, 1975. It was a game short on penalties and long on up-and-down-the-ice action, yet we don't encourage that sort of game in the NHL. Why the hell not?

I have a two-pronged suggestion that will make hockey big league again:

First, a fight should mean both players get tossed out for the game; any future fight should bring a two-week suspension, a third one banishment for the season.

Second, we should get rid of the rule that allows a penalized player back on the ice if a goal is scored against his team. Make him serve his full two minutes. The rule was only brought in because the Montreal Canadiens of old would often score two and sometimes three goals with the man advantage. A full two minutes will, like Samuel Johnson's man who knows he is to be hanged in a fortnight, "concentrate (the player's) mind wonderfully."

There may be unintended consequences of these improvements to deal with. For example, banning fighters for the rest of the game may give rise to some goon getting into a fight with an opposition star just to get him out of the game. The solution to this is that, if in the opinion of the referee the fight was deliberately started and the other player was simply defending himself, the aggressor gets sent off alone.

Why do I waste my time worrying about this? I'm only a former hockey fan who lived and died with the Montreal Canadiens but who has matured enough to see that fighting badly degrades the game. Watching fights and being forced to watch and listen to Don Cherry, Bob Cole, Ron MacLean, and the worst of the lot, Harry Neale has changed me from a man who watched every game available to one who only watches them as a social obligation. When you really think about it, as games are played today with the unbelievable skills demonstrated on the ice, watching a game should be sheer pleasure without a barbarity no other game would permit to be part of the regular fare.

The Manly Art of Self-Defence

I was, like most kids I knew, a boxing fan when I was growing up. I cheered for the "Brown Bomber" Joe Louis, "a credit to the race he represents." Then there was the best "pound for pound" fighter, Sugar Ray Robinson. And Tony Zale, Carmen Basilio, Rocky Graziano and the best, Rocky Marciano, who retired undefeated and stayed retired only to die in a plane crash while still a young man.

But I had an epiphany in 1960. The reigning heavyweight champion, Floyd Patterson, had been upset by a Swede named Ingemar Johansson, and in March 1961 they fought again. Patterson avenged his loss of nine months prior, and I will never forget the scene of Johansson lying on the canvass with just his foot twitching. I had never thought of boxing like that before. This wasn't the "manly art of self-defence" at all—this was inflicting concussions, each one of which damaged the brain. Johansson wasn't just beaten—he was injured. I thought back to when I was in the boxing finals at St. George's School for Boys. I was about ten at the time and up against a slightly younger Denis Stead, but I was so overmatched that I was hit with everything but the ring post. The headmaster, John Harker, had to call my dad to come and get me. But Denis and I remained friends, and I don't suppose I thought about that match much until that second Patterson-Johansson fight.

George Orwell once made the observation, "Serious sport has nothing to do with fair play. It is bound up with hatred, jealousy, boastfulness, disregard of all rules and sadistic pleasure in witnessing violence: In other words it is war minus the shooting." He was right. Now we have "ultimate fighting" which permits punching, wrestling, kicking and whatever else comes to mind, and we, as a society, wonder why the world is bent on murdering everything that moves. We wonder that as we watch TV and see men—hell, women too—trying to maim one another, mostly for the gain of the promoters and the advertisers. We're violent animals and it will be our undoing—and it all starts when the first punch is thrown at home, in the bar, or on the TV screen.

Thoughts the Day the Roof Blew Off

W e're told that Vancouver needs a new BC Place Stadium, the edifice locally known as "the Dome." Moreover, we're told that we the people should pay for it. I don't think so. I recognize the need for government to help with some entertainments such as the symphony and visual arts centres and the like, but I have trouble equating them with a stadium for hugely valuable franchises that hire overpaid jocks to peddle their wares in.

At the same time I don't entirely buy the argument that taxpayers in general should not have to pay for matters that happen in Vancouver. People from all over the province come to this city and use the facilities here. For example, the Vancouver General Hospital, which gets more tax money per capita than, say, Prince George or Kamloops, must have sympathetic funding from general revenue because in addition to being Vancouver's hospital it is a referral hospital and used as such for the entire province. Thus, everyone should pay for its operation.

In replacing the Dome, the example we should be looking to is San Francisco. Candlestick Park in that city was built in 1960 largely with public money and became a glowing example of Mair's Axiom I that says, "You make a serious mistake in assuming that people in charge know what the hell they're doing." It was located in the windiest part of the Bay Area, it was too large and too far away, and the sun shone in the outfielders' eyes; a new stadium was obviously needed.

Three times the Giants put a proposition to the public to use public money to build a new one; three times it failed. At last they were forced to look for private funds, and they found Pacific Bell. The new group recognized that you don't need eighty-thousand seats when you'll never fill them and that forty-thousand was just right, so a new, smaller ballpark now called AT&T Park was built in 1999. It was completed ahead of time and on budget. This was how it was funded: A $170 million loan from the Chase Manhattan Bank, $70 million from the sale of charter seat licences, $102 million from the sale of naming rights, sponsorships and other sources, and $15 million in tax increment financing by the city's redevelopment agency. Now everyone is happy, including the San Francisco Giants and the citizens of the Bay Area. The Giants' management are especially happy as they fill the park regularly.

The lesson? Let those who need a stadium build it and run it. David Braley, the owner of the Lions, wants to take over the Dome and deal with such improvements as are necessary including, I believe, building a new one. So sell the stadium to Mr. Braley. In short, let professional sports and their fans pay for their playpens.

Another Tigerish Thought

CBS golf commentator David Feherty relates a much-travelled anecdote that gives a glimpse of just how good Tiger Woods really is. Tiger is playing the eighteenth fairway at Firestone Country Club with Ernie Els and has buried his ball in some really nasty rough about forty yards behind Ernie. They are tied at this point, and Els is in the middle of the fairway. Tiger is one hundred eighty-four yards from the green with two big oak trees in the way. It couldn't look much worse for him.

Tiger takes his pitching wedge and unloads a vicious swing. Dirt and grass explode up around him. The ball arcs up over the trees, goes past the flag and rolls back into gimme territory. Els, who had been looking smug up to this point, is caught on an open mike saying, "Fuck me!"

Feherty said "I could have spent fifteen minutes describing that shot and not done as good a job as Ernie Els did with two words."

Tiger Woods has just won another tournament. Big surprise, huh? What shouldn't be a surprise is that he donated the winning purse of $1.35 million to the Tiger Woods Foundation (TWF). In fact, it was the eighth Target Gold Tournament that Tiger had sponsored—all the proceeds also going to the Fund—and the third he's won. He also donates fees paid for special appearances. I have no idea how much is in the pot but I've heard numbers like 75 million. Tiger is so supportive of this fund that he cancelled a place in an important tournament to attend a TWF dinner function. What does the Tiger Woods Foundation do? Two things: organizes education programs to enhance the learning processes for youth and sponsors year-round mentoring and/or tutoring programs. The accent isn't on golf but on youngsters in need, especially in inner cities.

At the age of thirty-one, Tiger has won thirteen major tournaments, leaving him five short of the eighteen that Jack Nicklaus piled up over his entire career. In doing this we have seen a man whose brilliance and determination has literally spooked his opponents, leaving some unable to compete again as they once did. The great Scottish player Colin Montgomerie played with him in the 1997 Masters, Tiger Woods' first "major" win. After watching Woods go four over par on the first nine then come back with a six under thirty on the back nine, Montgomerie, who had belittled the hoopla around Woods, was suddenly a believer! A couple of years ago in the British Open at St Andrews, Montgomerie, playing one group ahead of Woods, was in contention until Tiger ate him alive on the back nine. When interviewed after the Tiger win, Montgomerie said, "If the man behind you only needs to 'par in' to win, the very last person you want that man to be is Tiger Woods."

Tiger Woods' victory in the Buick Invitational on January 28, 2007, was his seventh time in a row on the PGA Tour. The record is eleven set by Byron Nelson in 1945. As Woods himself has pointed out, Byron did his all in one year and he didn't sit out any tournaments as Tiger did. Moreover, Woods had lost three non-PGA events within his PGA streak. And Tiger did not go on to make it eight.

I suppose it's because we all love streaks that the media gets on this sort of kick, but they have a problem examining the matter closely. Nelson's achievement was outstanding—no doubt on that score. It must be noted, though, that the competition was diluted by reason of World War II, from which Nelson was exempt for health reasons. However, even after the "boys" came home in 1946, Nelson won six tournaments, so while some of the tarnish is off his eleven-straight record, he was a magnificent golfer. In fact, I actually watched him play twice—once during the war when he went on tour with a who-can-ever-forget Jug McSpaden, and I saw him again in the fifties in an exhibition at Point Grey with Leroy Goldsmith, Stan Leonard and Ernie Brown. He was superb.

But there is a salient point to be made. No one has faced the competition Tiger does. In Nelson's time there was no European tour nor was there any Asian tour, and there were perhaps half a dozen players who could beat him on one of his rare "off days." Tiger has a field full of stiff competition, as the Buick Open demonstrated. In Nelson's day, the Ryder Cup with the UK was laughable so easily and often did the US win; today the European team is clearly dominant over the USA. And as I write this, the two top players in the world are Americans Jim Furyk and Tiger—but seven of the next eight are from elsewhere!

Jack Nicklaus claims that in his day the competition was stiffer than today, what with Palmer, Player, and Trevino breathing down his neck. He's talking nonsense and he knows it. There are modern equivalents to those fine players, the difference being that Tiger has driven them into the ground, both physically and mentally.

One can only be the best of his era and Nelson, for a couple of years, was that. Ben Hogan dominated his era as Nicklaus did for a few years. Nicklaus was the best of his. The fact is that no one— Bobby Jones, Nelson, Hogan, Palmer or Nicklaus—dominated the game as Tiger Woods has done, is still doing and will likely continue doing for some years to come.

We are all lucky to be alive to watch this remarkable man on the course and off.

Tiger Woods: great golfer, great humanitarian and, dare I say it, a great man.

PART IX

Small Heresies

What the Bleep Is Going On Here?

Here is what my *Merriam Webster Online Dictionary* has to say about that "bleep" word, "fuck":

Function: Verb
Etymology: Akin to Dutch *fokken* to breed (cattle), Swedish dialect *fókka* to copulate
Date: Circa 1503

intransitive verb
1. *usually obscene*: Copulate
2. *usually vulgar*: Mess–used with with

transitive verb
1. *usually obscene*: To engage in coitus with; sometimes used interjectionally with an object (as a personal or reflexive pronoun) to express anger, contempt or disgust.
2. *usually vulgar*: To deal with unfairly or harshly: Cheat or screw.

So there we have it: A perfectly clear English word with Germanic roots going back into the mists of time, a word that can be a transitive or intransitive verb, a noun, a gerund or a participle, not to mention expletive or interjection. Strangely, the online *Roget's Thesaurus* doesn't deal with the word in any form, which may be why people don't use *Roget* much anymore. But why is it considered a dirty word, perhaps only behind the two "c" words in the list of "naughties"?

One writer of yesterday, the unflappable Dorothy Parker, wasn't afraid. One of my favourite quotes came from Ms. Parker on Hallowe'en when she said "ducking for apples, change one letter and it's the story of my life." Explaining why she had not replied to a letter she said "too fucking busy…and vice versa."

I'm astonished at the lengths we go to in order to avoid using this four-letter word. I remember as a child reading a newspaper (yes, I did that as a child) and asking my father what "carnal knowledge" meant. He glared at me and spat out, "I don't know" and did so in a manner that he clearly believed I shouldn't know either. My father didn't like to hear the word in any of its manifestations though he is reputed to have liked what it means very much.

Today we use words like "frig" or "flipping" as cowardly cop-outs. I suppose "screw" is the most common synonym though I've often wondered how "screwing" became a double for sexual intercourse. I may have been doing it all wrong these many years past, but somehow I couldn't see any metaphorical connection between what I was doing and turning a screw. However, being a most unhandy sort of chap, I probably didn't have enough information to make an informed decision.

I make no attempt to make a list in any special way, but I suppose as synonyms that "piece of tail" and "piece of ass" are well up that list. Again I detect a problem, here one of geography. Now I don't deny that the "ass" or "tail" may be part of the manipulation that goes on with fucking, but in my view that hardly entitles it to synonymic equality.

"Getting laid" is a common phrase for fucking but doesn't this give undue prominence to the missionary method? Though God only knows I'm not experienced in this matter, either in performing the act or parsing sentences about it, it seems to me that this term has been forced by the real word into an archaic setting only to be used when all other words fail. It's interesting that, when we need to use the word "fuck" but think better of it, we clumsily say "they slept together" as if after-sex was the same as sex itself.

"Bonking" is positively British upper middle class as is "rogering." But I suppose "roger" is no worse than "restroom" or, for that matter, "john" for toilet, though come to think of it, toilet is a weasel word of its own. Perhaps we should use "crapper" since Thomas Crapper often gets the credit for giving us the modern flush toilet.

When I was a kid, "poontang" was the word used for the act of fucking, but in the interest of proper journalism I looked the word up in the *Urban Dictionary*, whatever the hell that is, and came up with this: "Poontang–noun inflected forms: Meaning 1. female genitalia; 2. sexual intercourse." It's thought to be Filipino in origin, which shows, I guess, what sophisticated and worldly lads we were. Jiggy jig or jigagig is sometimes heard these days but not often. It seems to be moving out of the list of "fucking synonyms." One of the more unique expressions I've heard in this regard comes from New Zealand where Kiwis often talk about a "slap and tickle." Today's political correctness would never allow the "slap" part, especially if the man was doing the slapping, and who wants to tickle anyway if you've already got her all the way into bed with her clothes off?

Oral sex has fared better since Bill Clinton moved the term "blowjob" off the proscribed list. I once observed on air that he had done young men a great service; never again would they have to explain to the object of their affections what a "blowjob" is. (You want me to put what where?)

When you think about it, there are a hell of a lot of synonyms to describe how all of us got started in life and, in all seriousness, I must

ask why? The word doesn't, of its own, imply any uncivilized conduct, so why do we shy away from its use while we freely use words
like "rape" when describing the act done by force? There certainly is
a coarseness about the way the word is often used but is it any coarser
than using the word "like" every three or four words? Or saying, "I
goes" and "she goes" when what is meant is "I said" and "she said"?
In fact, the word "fuck" is seldom used in an ungrammatical way, so
isn't a part of the disintegration of the English language evidenced by
the appalling misuse of "like" and "goes"? I've often said that if the
younger generations, instead of saying "like" said "fuck," the English
language would be better spoken.

Having stated the case for . . . er . . . f___, I now leave the debate
to wash my mouth out with soap.

What's in a Name?

I was christened, as we neatly called baptism in those days, Kenneth (after my father) Ralph (after a wealthy relative with one foot in the grave and another on a banana peel). I was to be called Ralph, but here's the rub—the name is, as with Ralph Vaughn Williams, Sir Ralph Richardson and actor Ralph Fiennes, pronounced RAFE. However, when I got to grade one at Maple Grove Elementary, the teachers called me Ralph so, being an ornery little bugger, I changed the spelling to R-a-f-e. All by myself, I did. I should have left well enough alone. When I was in high school, I used to explain it was pronounced like "rape" only with an "f" in it, which brought this reply from my late dear friend Fred Annett: "My name is Fred. It's like 'fuck' except there's an 'red' in it."

Eventually I changed the spelling legally—I was in politics by that time and this drew the attention of the press who saw something sinister in it and wouldn't let go for days. It must have been a slow news period. In any event, I still get every imaginable spelling and pronunciation, usually as if it had an accent so that it becomes Rafay.

Now, if my name was Admiral "The Honourable" Sir Reginald Aylmer Ranfurly Plunkett-Ernle-Erle-Drax (who really was a Royal Navy admiral—and, no, I'm not making this up!) and if I wanted to be called Ernle, I could understand how people might get a little impatient getting a formal name to call me. I could also understand how the civil service and those who keep records about us would be at sixes and sevens about how to handle it. What would his SIN card say? For sure he wouldn't be styled R.A.R.P.E.E.D. Let us assume, as happens with English folk of this ilk, he hates the name Reginald but keeps it so as to inherit his great-uncle's fortune. He's diddled if he doesn't bear that name on all formal government and private documents. But if they used his full name, they would need a bigger card or perhaps two cards, certainly two passports. Banks would probably recommend he use the local credit union. Amex would shuffle him off to Visa. In fact, one marvels that the Royal Navy put up with him and even made him an admiral.

Fortunately, I do not have such a name. I'm simply Kenneth Rafe I, II being my son and III being his elder son. But like poor old Ernle, I cannot get anyone I deal with to stop calling me Kenneth. I did get the Motor Vehicle Department to put Kenneth Rafe Mair on my licence and, because I never told them any different in the first place, Amex has me as Rafe Mair. Everything else comes in as "Dear Kenneth." It annoys me, too, parenthetically, when people I don't know—such as the gatekeeper in my chiropractor's office or my dentist's office—calls out, "Kenneth!" Not only am I not known as Kenneth, but what right does this employee of the person I employ have to call me anything but Mr. Mair? This is a new thing and it ought rapidly to be made an old thing.

But I digress. I thought I was all alone with this gnawing irritation about names, but one day I hosted a Channel 10 TV show with Steve Burgess and Terry O'Neil—great guys to have in a debate, incidentally, and somehow off-air the subject of names came up, and I learned that both are called by their second names and get very irritated by the same things I do. Like me, they spend precious moments of their diminishing time on this planet swearing, not always under their breath, at the latest misuse of their names.

Why is this so difficult to resolve in this computer age? As I write this, I'm listening to my iPod, which is tiny yet holds over four-hundred pieces of music. Can't the industry that has given us this and telephones that take pictures and teeny little chips that hold the entire Library of Congress not find a way for countries and companies to address me as Rafe Mair? Perhaps Terry, Steve and I should start a movement for fair play for those not called by their first names. Or we could change our names to Admiral Sir Reginald Aylmer Ranfurly Plunkett-Ernle-Erle-Drax I, Admiral Sir Reginald Aylmer Ranfurly Plunkett-Ernle-Erle-Drax II and Admiral Sir Reginald Aylmer Ranfurly Plunkett-Ernle-Erle-Drax III and let the bastards in Ottawa and Victoria deal with that!

The Trials and Tribulations
in the Life of a BC Writer

Please don't take the following as whining just because I raise a question coming out of my own experience. I have written seven books since 1994, this one being number eight. They have been kindly received by reviewers and sold well enough that publishers are always ready to go for another round.

I have learned from experience that a BC author must write as a labour of love, which I do. With one exception my royalties have been infinitesimal and I have never relied upon them for anything more than beer money or a plane ride to London.

I am happy to say that I have always been very well supported by smaller independent booksellers, which leads me to my point: book merchandising in Canada is dominated by one company, Indigo Books and Music Ltd, which owns the Chapters, Indigo, Coles and The Book Company stores, and I'm reliably informed that all decisions as to what to promote in the stores come from central Canada. This is bad news for writers from "the provinces."

I give you an example from my adventures with book number six. It was two weeks before Christmas and I was to sign books in an

Indigo store. My time there was to be two hours and I was told that there were thirty-five copies available. I raised my eyebrows a bit at this, and in the event I sold them all within the first hour. I asked the manager whether she would be getting more books. "No," she said, "that's certainly what I would do myself, but the decision is made in Toronto. In fact, I had to borrow fifteen books from another Chapters store to get what I had here today." I was almost speechless. "Do you mean then that two large stores will not have any of my books in stock for the last week before Christmas?" The answer was an embarrassed "yes." I checked with my publisher who told me that they could get books to these places within three days but that neither they nor the local store staff could make any move without an official purchase order from Chapters head office in Toronto.

This past Christmas I dropped into the Indigo-owned Book Company store in Park Royal in West Vancouver to see how my latest book was doing and to sign some if they wished. I scoured the store and finally found two copies spine-out alongside some of my past books under Canadiana. You literally had to get down on your hands and knees to see them. In a much more prominent location, under "New Books Non-Fiction," were three rows of a new book on Ontario political butterfly and car-parts heiress Belinda Stronach with two of the columns facing outwards! I had words with the manager but nothing was to change. In the end my book outsold Belinda's by about two to one in the BC market, despite the huge marketing advantage her book enjoyed in the province's dominant book chain. Nobody should have been surprised by this result. In downtown Toronto where the Indigo head office is located, local celeb Belinda no doubt has a higher profile than yours truly. But in BC where I have been building an audience since she was in knee socks, she is irrelevant. If Chapters-Indigo-The Book Company was responsive to BC buying patterns they would have placed my book three columns deep up front and hers spine out down on the bottom shelf.

I don't think my complaint is just my personal hysteria. I think that, as with all centralized programs in this country, unless it's big in Toronto or Montreal, it just doesn't matter. Monopolies are inherently evil and Chapters-Indigo is no exception. Indigo CEO Heather Reisman really ought to get on a plane, fly to a place named Vancouver and see that real people live there, people who would support local authors if they only knew where to find their goddamn books.

Care to Take a Flutter?

There is a lot of legalized gambling going on in this country and all forms have one thing in common: Someone who isn't in the game but runs it makes a piss pot full of money—at the consumer's expense. And as far as gambling goes, there's not much difference between the major stock markets and horse racing. The owner of the racetrack couldn't care less who wins because he gets his slice out of each bet no matter how the race turns out. If favourites win, it might encourage others to bet, but the fact remains that the consumer always loses even when he wins because the track owner and the government have taken their share up front.

So it is with the stock salesman. He's the middle man who snaps up a fee whether you have won or lost. And like the racetrack owner, your broker offers you incentives to play. While the horseman offers you different ways to lose your money with quinellas, daily doubles, exactors, trifectas and so on, the broker offers common stock, bonds, mutual funds and so on to encourage you to make "bets." But here's the rub: Even though he wears the best bespoke suits, $200 ties and silk underwear, the broker, like the horseman—or the Lotto Canada seller, for that matter—wants you to bet and bet often. It's helpful to track owners and brokers if their clients win often enough to keep coming back, but that's not because they like to see people win. The crucial part is that they *play*. The broker doesn't like the comparison with the horseman so he pretends to be part of the upper crust whereas, in fact, he's no better than a Third World lottery-ticket salesmen flogging hope to the poor or the man who runs the numbers racket in the Bowery. (I should say "used to run it" because that racket has been taken over by the government whose payoffs make the "numbers game" thugs look like Santa Claus by comparison.)

The theory behind mutual funds is that you participate in many companies running from the shaky to the sure thing, thus minimizing your chance of losses. However, they also minimize your chance of profits, though the salesman is not big on telling you that! With many mutual funds you're behind the eight ball from the start as the broker grabs his take off the top. Having said that, there are mutual funds that have done well. But here's the question you might ask yourself: Who do you think is paying for all those expensive and exotic trips that mutual fund management companies continually send their successful brokers on?

Let's take a closer look at buying and selling stock. As mentioned, it matters little to the broker what your stock does as long as you keep playing and keep the commissions rolling in. Let me illustrate. A couple of years ago Wendy and I, given our ages and what we wanted, instructed our broker to sell everything and put it in treasury bills. I was then, as I am even more since the recent crash, scared stiff of the market for many reasons. The US is the biggest debtor nation in the world where it once was the biggest creditor. And its biggest creditor today? China, for God's sakes! Oil will, in my opinion, go sky high—at this writing oil has hit $109 per barrel. Helmut Pastrick, the distinguished economist for BC Credit Unions, said that if it hit $100 all economic predictions are out the window. The Chinese economy, like the Japanese economy of twenty years ago, is in spite of the glitz based upon a foundation of quicksand. It's riding for a fall that, if it happens, will hit all of us—hard.

But the main reason Wendy and I wanted out of the market was to keep our capital secure. We didn't have much and wanted peace of mind much more than anticipated profits and feared losses. Our broker couldn't understand people who didn't want to make a profit but, much against his will, sold, all the time bleating that we were making a big mistake because "in the long run, et cetera, et cetera." I simply could not make him understand that I don't have a long run to recover from losses and that I needed my capital safely tucked away.

After we had sold out, our broker got heat from his superiors. "How come all that money is lying there when it could be out making commissions?" The pressure was on and we started to get phone calls. This was a "bull market" and he would put us only into the very safest investments, he said. Next thing we knew, little by little we were back in and feeling very stupid for abandoning our own instincts and listening to the securities tout. Of course, we were hardly back in when the type of stock we were in went into the toilet and we lost what for us was a lot of money. At that point so convinced were we that this was a good time to stand on the sidelines and watch that we sold out again and stayed out.

This is not a poor-Rafe-and-Wendy story because we were the ones who gave in to the pressure when we should have known better. What this is, however, is a statement of fact. Brokers make money out of an active portfolio and all else is of secondary importance. (By way of aside, let me tell you what happens if you complain when this kind of thing happens—the company uses its own in-house lawyer who talks to everyone involved and then, surprise! surprise! finds the broker and the company absolutely innocent!)

Let's suppose your broker tells you to buy a stock that his brokerage company is very high on. Does he say this is because independent researchers have investigated the stock? Not likely. What is more likely is that the brokerage house has underwritten the stock, meaning that they have paid for stock, kept a bundle for themselves and want the stock to go up so they can blow it off and cash in. In short, they want to move the risk from themselves to you and make a bundle in the process. Who better to raise the cash from but their clients? The concept of "conflict of interests" is unknown in the stocks and bonds business. Moreover, stocks salesmen simply do not understand that for some people—Wendy and me, for example—the preservation of capital is far more important than making money. We put peace of mind far ahead of potential profits.

Then there is the crime of "insider trading." The case most people know most about is the call made by Herb Doman to Russell Bennett in which Doman said that Louisiana Pacific was not going to buy Doman Industries and Bennett should dump his Doman shares before the news became public. This was bad business and no one can condone it, but it is child's play compared to what happens every day in the big kids' stock market.

First, there are the share options given to CEOs and directors. The game is that they accept options to buy shares with the base price being the selling price at the time they received the options. If the stocks go up, they simply redeem the options and sell the shares for, it's hoped, a handsome profit. Now think about this for a moment: Is any CEO or director going to call his options and sell them unless he knows that it's a good business move? And isn't it obvious that the only way he would know this would be through insider information?

There is also the common scam by which President Bush, among others, made a killing. Like most stock scams, it's simplicity itself. You take a company that, for example, makes widgets—a company that you control and whose stock is trading, let's say, at a dollar. You and your fellow executives issue yourselves a bundle of options to buy company stock at a dollar. You then get another company that you control (secretly of course) to offer to buy a million widgets. You make this wonderful news available to the public who immediately drive the stock up to $10; you call your options and sell them for a $9 profit per share. There's one more thing, of course—you must later announce, alas and alack, that the company that was to have bought the widgets quite suddenly went bankrupt before it could make payment.

Prosecutions for breach of insider information rules are rare and absolutely non-existent among the big boys and girls, whereas on the old Vancouver Stock Exchange, stock hucksters of this same kind were held in contempt and even sometimes charged. From my own unhappy experience I can tell you that most players in those stocks are gamblers. They know the game and don't care if a company is honest as long as it has a good "story" and that story runs the stock up so they can make money. In the words of W.C. Fields, "you cannot cheat an honest man." The VSE was, of course, a crap game where "investors" understood the rules or lack of them, but the public has been led to believe that the Toronto Stock Exchange, the New York Stock Exchange and other major players are run by pillars of honesty and moral rectitude. In fact, they are big time pickpockets.

Finally, let's blow to smithereens the notion that brokers are extremely well educated and spend most of their waking moments analyzing the companies whose shares they flog. If they know their stocks so well, why don't they ever advise their clients to sell short? (Selling short means you sell shares *you don't own* because you think they will go down, then buy them after they go down and pocket the difference.) Brokers don't do this because the stock market is supposed to be a jolly place where ne'er shall be heard a discouraging word of pessimism. Nortel, a glamour stock that went into the dumper and took a lot of folks with it, is a good example. Everyone knew after it went down the tube that it was overpriced, yet brokers kept getting clients to buy all the way down. Cut down your average cost, they said. The stock is sure to go back up sometime soon! In fact

—and this is the point—the bad things about Nortel were just as easy to see before it crashed, when it was the darling of the TSE, as they were with hindsight.

The central point is this: To the broker, be he Slippery Sam, the flogger of Consolidated Moose Turds, or the man in the three-piece suit in the exclusive club talking up a "blue-chip" stock, the name of the game is transactions for which they are paid commissions and making profits on stocks they themselves own. The guiding axioms are: 1) you don't have to be mad to be in the stock market—but it helps—and 2) always remember that to the broker it doesn't so much matter what the dice read; for him it's how many rolls you throw. If you must stay in the market, continually look at your stocks and ask yourself if you would buy them at their current prices. If you would, keep 'em; if you wouldn't, flog 'em as fast as you can, regardless of what your broker says.

A Flutter Too Far

I have always enjoyed taking a flutter on a horse or the turn-up of a card. When on a cruise, I often toss a few coins into the slot machines or play a bit of blackjack. In short, I don't oppose gambling on some moral basis. What I do say is that gambling has gone too far… way too far.

I remember when it was illegal to buy tickets on the Irish Sweepstakes, though I always had a ticket courtesy of a waiter in the bar of the Vancouver Club who sold them on the side. He might have been fired for this illegality had not the president and the board members also been amongst his customers. In those days one could get a licence for a charity bingo night, but such events were strictly controlled by the local police.

It was back in 1978 or thereabouts that Grace McCarthy presented a new lottery system to cabinet, a system that would be sponsored by the federal government with the revenues shared with the provinces. This was Lotto 6/49. I objected to it by saying that, as anyone who had gone to Mexico City would know, lotteries are a tax on the poor who see their distant-unto-invisible lottery chance as a way out of the ghetto. But it came, and after that came the charity casinos which begat the larger casinos with slot machines, until now we have the kind of grand casinos one only expected to see in Las Vegas or Atlantic City.

Gambling has become a cash cow for many communities as well as providing a nice little poke for the government. But what all of us as citizens tend to forget is that the game is fixed. If the bettor could make money, the casino would be out of business. You never see a casino employee come along to load up the slot with money! Moreover, the backbone of any casino is not the high roller at the craps table but the player of the twenty-five-cent slot machine.

I suppose it's now too late to ask if we're a people who want to continue to see our taxes, in effect, reduced by the amount the poor pump into our friendly slot machines. But at least we should pause and think, then feel ashamed at what we've allowed to happen in the name of a little bit of fun.

Boxing Week

The October arrival of Santa Claus and the constant, ever-building mercantile propaganda before Christmas has got to make one feel more than a bit grinchy. Last year I thought that Christmas Eve would be a good time to go to my barber in Park Royal North, get my ears lowered and beard trimmed. I couldn't get near the place in my car. The only doable course would have been to walk there, but I live in Lions Bay!

By way of aside, here's a wonderful little story that's making the rounds: A little boy visits Santa with his dad.

"Santa," says little boy, "you remember how I saw you last week at the Hudson's Bay store?"

"Of course," Santa replies.

"Are you really coming to my house on Christmas Eve like you promised?"

"Of course I am," says Santa.

"Will you have your sled and eight reindeer plus Rudolph?"

"You can depend on me," says Santa.

"Well," says the lad, "will you be landing on the lawn or the roof?"

"Definitely the roof," the jolly old soul replied.

"Well, then," says the persistent lad, "would you mind getting my frisbee off the roof while you're at it?"

And the advertising folks really know how to piss you off. Boxing Day used to be a single day where the "better-off" gave to the poor, but it's become Boxing Week, seven or eight days of massive sell-offs to the patient buyer.

Last Christmas evening I was watching a football game with my son-in-law and his dad when we began discussing the new big digital TV sets, and my son-in-law brought up the price of these things.

"I paid $2,500 for mine," said Larry, and his dad smiled and reported that he had paid only $2,300 for his. Just then an ad came on the TV offering, in its Boxing Week (what a nauseating term) Sale, the same set for $1999.

So I've seen the light. I'm about to join the Eastern Orthodox Church. Quite apart from the fact that as a lapsed Anglican any port in the storm will do, look at the money I'll save by celebrating Christmas on January 6! As Henry IV, King of France, said as he abandoned his Protestant commitment to return to Catholicism, "Paris is worth a mass." I say, what's a change of religion when there's money to be saved?

Do Not Open Until Xmas

Every Christmas for a very long time now our "higher purpose persons" (to use the late Denny Boyd's marvelous phrase) have busied themselves taking all indicia of Christianity out of the otherwise jolly picture. In schools nativity scenes and Christmas carols are swept away by misguided do-gooders who, though they claim to be speaking for minority groups, never seem to be part of them. "Canada is not a Christian country!" they cry—which is true but irrelevant. The event is about the celebration of Jesus's birth, an event not much noticed by Christians in earlier years. While Christianity is not our national religion any more than Zoroasterism is, Christmas has become a national day of considerable importance to all Canadians of every conceivable background.

It has become many things to many people. Some Christians, though not all by any means, celebrate December 25 as a holy day. Most people, including I daresay most Christians—at least the nominal once-or-twice-a-year variety—celebrate it as a season of goodwill. And for most Canadians it is a wonderful, joyous time of year, a time for youngsters, a short time dedicated to friends and family not seen very often, a time for loved ones to get together to renew their love. People of all faiths say Merry Christmas to each other and to utter strangers.

In our house it was presents right after breakfast as Dad would light the sparklers. Then it would be off to church for what for my father was his only visit there of the year. He would be some pissed off if, for some reason, what he regarded as the family pew (the second from the front on the left side) was occupied by others. As my mother used to actually make it there for Easter too, Dad thought this confirmed our prescriptive rights to that particular pew.

As it was for most people who professed even some wispy connection to Christianity, Christmas in those days was a very special day for our family. It was a wonderful time for kids and adults alike because around this special day people from all faiths and walks of life suddenly were nice to one another. It isn't always that way, of course. Sometimes, in the immortal words of Yogi Yorgesson in his famous spoof "I Yust Go Nuts at Christmas," "someone slugs Uncle Ben" and all hell breaks loose. Sometimes it's a struggle between whose folks will have the big dinner this year, a problem exacerbated if one set of "folks" can't stand the guts of the other.

But here's what our self-proclaimed champions of neutralizing Christmas simply do not understand. To the chagrin of many Christians, Christmas has broadened its appeal to almost everyone. Legends old and new have blended into a sort of super festival. Old Saint Nicholas now finds himself led by Gene Autry's Rudolph, plus the eight of old, or so say millions of kids and who will tell them they're wrong?

The nativity scene is not some sort of fundamentalist Christian form of proselytizing the faith but a moment of great religious significance to some and just beauty and peace to others. To some it means nothing at all and that doesn't matter. "O Come, All Ye Faithful," which only reaches its true majesty when sung in Latin, "Silent Night" and "Joy to the World" have long since been joined by "White

Christmas," "Jingle Bells" and "Frosty the Snow Man." Does it matter that these songs widen the scope of celebrating a message of peace?

Of course, there are lots of downsides to Christmas, which for many has become a ten-day period of spending and eating and drinking too much. It's become far too commercialized—though just what the right amount would be is never clear. But surely these bad things just demonstrate that Christmas is what you want to make of it.

Many Christians would like to redeem Christmas, seize it from the infidels and get it back inside the church. Good luck! The English language will reclaim the word "gay" in its true meaning before that happens. Christians, in accordance with Jesus's constant plea for peace and understanding, must make the best of it and stop complaining that others are ruining their holy day. It remains for them to celebrate or not as they see fit. Non-Christians should not fear to be reminded about the origins of the great feast.

Merry Christmas, happy Chanukah, best of the season and may we all be around this time next year to continue the never-ending debate.

Hurray for Modern Electronics!

I've been using a computer since 1982 and I still don't understand a single thing about it. I get by—most of the time—but I'm damned if I know how and why things go wrong and I sure as hell don't know how to fix them.

I went online about ten years ago—maybe a little less. But in those days it took two or three steps to get on the net and I could never remember in what order. Of course, there wasn't nearly the information available on it that there is now. It was a novelty as when TV first came into your house. You could visit the Smithsonian Institute or the British Museum, but you couldn't get important information such as where was Tiger in the current tournament. (Silly question, really, he's on top!) When it became easy, I started to get information that was really helpful. This became especially true after Google came along. The trouble is there is now far too much information available and searches are taking up far too much time, so perhaps it won't be long before my library has some practical use again. The parts of it that have sunk into disuse are my handy little *Concise English Dictionary*, my *Roget's Thesaurus*, *Bartlett's Familiar*

Quotations and the like. I miss thumbing through those beer-stained pages and I haven't given them away. Still, the web's a pretty good deal when you remember just two or three words in a quote and you can key them in and get an instant answer.

I must admit I don't know how I wrote in the years before 1981. Although my IBM Selectrix was a pretty good machine, as I am a pick and pecker, it was still a chore big time. But since 1981 I have written God-only-knows how many editorials and articles plus eight books on a word processor. I guess I must give it its due. Now, goddammit, how do I get that bloody thing unlocked?

My new cellphone is quite beyond me. I want one that lets me phone out. I don't care if it doesn't receive calls. I don't want to store numbers and I sure as hell don't want it to take pictures, get on the internet, send and receive emails and play songs in my ear. I just want to phone out to Wendy if I'm going to be late and to the BCAA if my car stops.

I have always disliked telephones. I've always considered that calls I make are important and those I receive are, for the most part, nuisances and unwarranted intrusions into my privacy (unless they were from a girl, of course). For the longest time I wouldn't get a cellphone because they bite back at me. I used Wendy's phone once and in turning it off I evidently kept my finger on the button too long and she had to call the phone people to get it right again. I don't use my new cellphone for the simple reason that, despite all the careful and patient instructions, I simply can't make it work. When I press the red button, the same one that turns it off, too many things happen—flashing lights, moving logos, strange instructions, menus. It's an electronic kaleidoscope! Then you must punch the numbers you want with fingers that are twice as big as the key so you screw up. Now what? Through all that bullshit again! Then when it does work, no one's home!

Not long ago I read an article suggesting that the Blackberry is science gone way too far, and it warmed my heart. It was by one of those people who writes about the very latest in electronic gadgetry and compares one toy with another. I've become a bit more interested in this sort of stuff since I got an iPod—except I now have three of them and Wendy has another. I believe that every time I called with yet another problem the Apple people had a general alarm sounded so that no service person would have to deal with me more than once. Being utterly illiterate when it comes to computer-ese, I would drive both the helper and myself to tears as I tried to relate what my problem was. One day I told the Apple lady that I'd only had their iPod a couple of days and it wouldn't work any more. "What kind of a product is that?" I thundered as only a former Consumer Affairs Minister could do.

"Have you tried recharging it?" she asked sweetly.

"Oh, they need recharging, huh?" was my brilliant response.

I went back to the computer in full blush after my gaffe, but my iPod simply wouldn't recharge even though I did everything she had told me.

Back to the phone and another soothing and understanding female voice. "Have you got it plugged into the computer?" she asked (sweetly again).

Now I was pissed off. "Of course," I replied. "I put the socket of the white cord you told me about into the iPod just where you told me to." God, these so-called experts can be stupid, I thought.

The "sweet" lady then asked, "Is the cord you have put into the iPod also connected with that wire with the blue light on the end that goes into the computer?"

"Into the computer, you say? Babble, babble, babble. Thanks for your time."

Shaw Cable has, I think, the same system in place to deal with me that Apple has. Short straw gets Rafe next time he phones to say, "My TV is on the fritz!" I usually get a man when I phone and he has the patience of Job. He knows that I not only don't know what I'm doing but that I don't understand the lingo either.

"What seems to be the trouble, Mr. Mair?"

"Well," I say, "at the beginning I had sound and no picture. Then as I worked my way through the possibilities the remote control offers, I wound up with a picture and no sound. Now I have no sound, no picture and a screen full of coloured snow. I then gave the remote control my Oscar Peterson technique for fixing computers and remote controls—I played with all the numbers in the hope (like when the monkeys hit the keys so often they came up with the Bible) that my TV would miraculously work again. Except I didn't get the Bible, just a friggin' TV that won't work."

The patient Shaw person then walks me through the steps needed and I get picture and sound. "But," I weakly tell the repairman, "it really isn't my fault. All I want is a clicker that turns the TV on and off, changes channels and permits me to change the volume. I don't want menus, favourite channels, two pictures on the screen and that crap, just the simple necessities." I get patronizing sympathy, which reminds me of both my age and utter incompetence with electronic devices and the like. Of course, I must sadly conclude that such simple devices went out with the 1953 Studebaker Champion I once owned. Both should come back into vogue, if you ask me.

But as the man in that article said, the Blackberry (and the remote control, I would add) is science gone too far, way too far, so that instead of being helpful it's a gigantic pain in the ass. But for all this, I have learned to love my iPod and as I type this, I'm listening to the haunting refrain of Dinah Shore's "The Gypsy," popular back in '46, I believe. Now, however, I have three 2GB iPods and Wendy has one!

I have about a thousand CDs, which are a bugger to store. Any arrangement means that sometimes I must get down on my hands and knees to see what I have, which with my badly arthritic knees just doesn't happen. My stepdaughter and her mate came to my rescue and gave me five CD holders holding 250 CDs each that I can only describe as being photo albums for CDs. Now all are accessible, and as I filled up my first iPod, I found songs I didn't know I had. I knew very little, for example, about Foster & Allen, an Irish folk song duo, but after I stuck their "Maggie" on the iPod and immediately recognized it, I ordered a Foster & Allen CD. I also found the John McCormack version of "Londonderry Air." How the hell I got that I'll never know and there's Kate Smith singing "God Bless America." Lots of ABBA, the Mamas & the Papas and Connie Francis, all of whom helped me stay sane as I brought up stepchildren in the midst of the "musical" horrors that marked the '70s and '80s.

I find that over the years I've accumulated a huge number of Ella numbers, "Jazz at the Philharmonic" concerts (including the very first one), masses of King Cole, Benny Goodman and God-only-knows how many Lionel Hamptons. Benny Carter is there and so is Thelonious Monk, George Shearing and oodles of Oscar Peterson. There are a dozen Frankie Laine CDs and probably the same number of Sinatra from his early days when he could sing. But I made a fascinating discovery as I filled my number one iPod with about 425 bits of music: I had a hell of a lot of stuff stuck in compilations that I didn't know about! It was painstaking work but what fun as I uncovered gem after gem. In fact my iPods have made me into a music sleuth.

When I was about eleven or twelve my Aunty Lo gave me a record—78 rpms, of course—of a trumpeter named Sonny Dunham doing "Memories of You." I loved it and wore it out on the old wind-up gramophone we had at camp. I forgot all about this until I got my iPod and starting thinking about stuff I'd liked as a kid. I remembered this song so vividly—could it be found? Was it as good as I remembered? I checked in stores in London, New York and San Francisco. Nothing. Then the Internet. Nothing. Then someone told me he thought Dunham had played for Glen Gray and the Casa Loma Orchestra, and sure enough, on a CD called *Mostly 1939* there was Sonny Dunham with "Memories of You." And it was better than I remembered! Some months later I was on Dal Richards' show, *Dal's*

Place on 600AM in Vancouver. (For those who don't know, Dal is one of Canada's great bandleaders and still is fully booked at the age of 90!) He flattered me by agreeing that this was indeed the best trumpet solo he'd ever heard.

I love tweaking my iPod—taking out this and adding that is a lot of fun. Moreover, it's taken over my car's CD player as I've got that little attachment that lets me plug the iPod into the cigarette lighter and play out on an empty FM station. So where am I then? I hate cellphones and TV remote control devices but love my iPods. What the hell, one out of three isn't all that bad!

PART X

The City by the Sea

Where Will It All End?

I chair an ongoing series of public meetings put on by the Greater Vancouver Regional District, now Metro Vancouver. These meetings deal with all manner of things including transportation, the environment, the cost of land and so on. I open each meeting with this question: Where will it all end? This is not just a question that doesn't attract solutions, it doesn't even attract responses! But it *is* a question that we will have to respond to and answer before we go much further.

I don't imagine there's a city of any size in Canada that doesn't have a transit problem. At the base of those problems are two irrefutable facts: People want to drive their cars and, as was so well put in that marvelous baseball novel *Shoeless Joe* by BC writer W.P. Kinsella (which became the movie *Field of Dreams*), "Build it and they will come." Unhappily that prediction also applies to the building of more highways to accommodate more people. More room for motorists brings more cars, which in turn brings more highways. It is these two facts that have city planners and politicians tearing their hair out. And to that must be added the politician's nightmare—the unforeseen consequences of your actions.

I suspect that most Canadian cities, while not all having precisely the same problems arising from their geography and demographic changes, are dealing with just what Greater Vancouver is dealing with. Back in the '50s Vancouver (actually it was the BC Electric Railway) decided to get rid of the street car/interurban system and go for buses. (Toronto, though pressured to do the same thing, had the sense to keep its streetcars.) Thus we were committed to what we thought was a "modern day" system, whereas we had opted for a system that was outdated from the start. Unintended consequences, namely an even worse transit situation, reared its ugly head. Then in 1968 the city fathers and mothers decided that there would be no freeways built. They patted themselves on the back for their brilliant decision but neglected to come up with an alternative solution. By the 1980s it was apparent that not only was there no transportation system but there was no plan. The unintended consequence of that council's decision was chaos.

It is not my theme here to pick and choose what the best way to handle things might be. London charges a user fee for cars that come into the city, a solution that, for geographical reasons, might not work elsewhere. Some cities are ideally suited to a rail system while others are not. London has what we do not—superb transportation from bedroom communities to downtown, though it must be remembered that London started this system over a hundred years ago and still has to establish new Underground lines and these are hugely expensive.

What the worry should be for all Canadian urban dwellers is this: Where does it all end? No matter what transit systems you choose, they are usually outdated either immediately or at least within a few years because, the system having been built, people do in fact come. This means places must be found for newcomers to live, putting ever greater pressure on adjacent farmland and tending toward tall ugly tenement buildings. Once you have housed all these newcomers, you find that, damn them, they breed and import relatives and friends, so soon we need yet another transit system or a huge overhaul of the one we have.

Where will it all end?

The Vancouver Club After Forty Years

(Originally published in *BC Business* Magazine)

The Vancouver Club, much parodied as the home of old men sleeping off a lunch full of gin, is an institution in our province. Most of the high and the mighty were and are members. Both my father and one of my grandfathers were members, and before I became a member in June 1966, I would sometimes go there for lunch with my dad. I didn't know whether to laugh or tremble at the atmosphere. It made a mausoleum look exciting by comparison.

My dad put me up for membership in 1964, but when my name was approved about a year later, I couldn't afford the entrance fee or the monthly dues. It usually took four years for a name to come up again, but there must have been an increased death rate that year because in June 1966 my name came up for the second time. Under the rules it was now or never: If I didn't sign up, I would be off the list and forced to join the Terminal City Club where, hard though this is to believe, insurance salesmen and that sort were welcome! (It was said that, when a prospective member got on the waiting list at the Vancouver Club, he joined the adjacent Terminal City Club and counted the times the flag was at half mast at the

Vancouver Club indicating that a death had created an opening. When sufficient lowered flags had been noted, the prospective member kissed the upstart Terminal City Club goodbye and sauntered over to the Vancouver Club with a cheque book in hand.)

I had a wife and four small kids when my number came up that second time and I couldn't see how I could afford it. However, my law partners, seeing an opportunity to get a better class of clients (they never materialized!) agreed that the firm would pay the initiation fee and reasonable expenses—quite a gesture considering one of those partners was a Jew and there was an unwritten rule that, with the exception of converts to the Anglican faith, Jews were distinctly not welcome as members. This was because, as my dad explained, they would take over the club! Then it happened. Enough had become enough for Lieutenant-Governor Walter Owen and the chief justice of the Court of Appeal, John Farris, who in 1977 proposed Nathan Nemetz, a Jew, for membership. No board would refuse this powerful application, thus the Vancouver Club at long last rid itself of this disgraceful unwritten rule. Mr. Nemetz was a man of extraordinary talents who himself would later become chief justice of the Court of Appeal. All races and religions are now welcome.

In 1966 the Vancouver Club was an English-style men's club, dark and cheerless, a place where voices were soft and a display of mirth beyond the hint of a smile was frowned upon. Women guests— only allowed at dinner (escorted by a member, of course)—were not permitted to enter the club through the main entrance but only via a side door! One night I stood waiting to be admitted with my wife outside the Ladies Door in a downpour of epic proportions, so I said to hell with it and we went through the front door. The hall porter asked if he could have a brief word with me and in hushed tones reminded me of the "ladies door" rule.

The men's loo had ancient and enormous "made in Barrhead, Scotland," urinals where you could hide almost your entire body from prying eyes. They, alas, went out in 1973. (This reminds me of a story of Lord Birkenhead who, when coming back from dinner, would go into a famous London club that had refused him membership in order to relieve himself. One night the hall porter said, "Milord, this is a private club, you know," whereupon Birkenhead replied, "Oh, is it that, too?")

On the main floor of the Vancouver Club was the reading room—deep chairs and all the right magazines and papers such as *The London Times, Punch, The Illustrated London News* and, oh heresy, *The New Yorker*. This was where, after a liquid lunch, the cream of Vancouver's business community slept it off before wobbling back to the office. They would return to the club at five o'clock sharp and repair promptly to the men's bar on the third floor to top the day off with a few drinks for the road. To this day the men's bar has lockers where members kept their liquor, and there's a lovely story of a new member who, shown to his locker, discovered it had a bottle of his favourite Scotch therein. What a lovely gesture, he thought. I wonder how they knew my brand? As time passed, the bottles seem to go faster than he thought his consumption warranted but there was always a fresh supply when needed. One day as he was reaching in for his jug, the man next to him said in a higher pitch than the club preferred, "So you're the bastard that's been into my Scotch!" Our new member hadn't realized that until you attained some seniority, you shared lockers! I've had locker number 13 for forty-one years now and though I don't drink hard liquor any more, I still keep the locker and some hootch in it against the times I take a guest up.

This third floor bar had a large round table where anyone was welcome, but one senior member, George Clark, would come into the bar at 5:15 precisely and take his usual seat at the table. One day a new member, having been told that the round table had no special places, sat down in the chair that George usually sat in. We all watched and waited for what was bound to be an interesting moment. At 5:15 on the dot George came in, walked up to his usual chair and just stood there. "Oh," said the young man, "is this your chair?" George just stared at this interloper who then vacated the chair and the bar. There were members and then there were members, so to speak.

The dining room on the second floor was and remains as fine as I've ever seen and I've seen some of London's finest. The tuxedoed waiters, the head waiter in tails (as is the cue man in the billiard room), the best of food and wines mark the Vancouver Club as world class.

By the early '90s the Vancouver Club began to have the financial woes that beset most downtown clubs, so in 1994 it absorbed the University Club—the male members, that is. I was furious and, breaking my vow of political silence, wrote the board to remind them that, if they allowed women members into the Vancouver Club, this absorption of the University Club would be unnecessary. I had nothing against the University Club; it was just that the Vancouver Club didn't need to do this if they dragged themselves out of the Edwardian era and welcomed women members. My letter was acknowledged but no more.

But the issue of female members simmered like a peat fire until, in 1997, a motion at the annual general meeting to amend the constitution so as to allow women members was tabled. Unfortunately, it didn't receive the necessary 75 percent vote, and many members, including me, promptly resigned. I, however, had erred by dating my resignation April 1, the beginning of the next month, and I received a call from the president, Peter Manson, saying that I was a member until June 30 whether I liked it or not so would I please help him get a new special motion passed? (By way of aside, in my letter of resignation I asked what kind of stupid club would require 75 percent to change its bylaws? When Peter replied that this was because of the new Society Act brought in by the NDP, I suddenly felt that devastating blow that comes with gross embarrassment. "No, Peter," I said, "it was I as a Socred minister who brought in the new Society Act in 1978." When the press found out, it was a pretty good laugh on me and deservedly so.)

A special meeting was called. The telephone campaign went into high gear, and on the appointed night members were lined up right around the block. The new resolution passed by a massive margin. Our troubles were over, so we thought, for now the ladies would break the doors down to get in. But it didn't happen. We hadn't realized the extent of the smouldering anger and it took a couple of years before the ladies came. But come in they did at last, bringing with them the Georgian Club, an old and prestigious club for ladies.

By the mid-'90s the "Young Turks" had finally taken over the board of directors from the "Old Farts" and things started to happen. Excellent modern exercise facilities were added. The old reading room—to the horror of the "Old Farts"—was expanded to include a solarium and became a very popular bar and grill where there is often live entertainment such as jazz combos. Soon the young business people and professionals began to arrive in considerable numbers. The old Vancouver Club would never be the same again—and thank God for that. This is a new, modern club that is fun to be part of—hell, it even has a barbershop now. The place, if it doesn't quite jump, is alive and happy. With casual dress everywhere but the dining room, there is a new, fresh air about the 117-year-old Vancouver Club and, though my dad and grandfather are no doubt spinning in their graves at this massive *lese majeste*, I love it.

Forty years on, the Vancouver Club has come a long way, and my fellow "Old Farts" who quit because of the modernization don't know what they're missing and, I hate to say it, we who stayed don't much miss them.

Buying Things

I am not a Luddite opposed to all change, but I am concerned about my community and how we buy our necessaries and non-necessaries, and in my lifetime I have seen many changes in marketing. Whether these changes were necessary is for another debate, but what has happened is a spinning-wheel effect wherein the mode of merchandising has all but come full circle.

When I was a lad, shops—with the exception of department stores—stood on their own. We went to James Inglis Reid for meat and fish (including kippers), Harkley and Haywood for fishing tackle, Sweet 16 or Saba's for ladies clothes and Purdy's for chocolates and our morning coffee. (Mr. Forrester always had chocolate "Gold Medallions" for us kids.)

Come the '50s we saw Canada's first shopping mall (I leave it to you whether this deserves praise or blame) at Park Royal now Park Royal South, the key to which was Woodward's Store, now defunct. The mall seemed such a good idea at the time. It was one-stop shopping where you could complete your shopping list, have your haircut and even have a root canal. And it was dry shopping, a serious concern and a big plus on the West Coast. The trouble was that it didn't age well, and the cost of rent kept a lot of small specialty stores out.

I don't think that Vancouverites ever really took to the mall as they have to the new "village" type shopping centre next to Park Royal South. Here you can shop at a leisurely pace and have open-air lunch with a glass of wine while you "people watch." The stores reflect the open-air atmosphere that we want both in the way they look and the attitude of the workers. It's also likeable for what it is *not*—a place for kids to frolic and old farts to play checkers. Thus the future has become the past. Now if only Purdy's and Mr. Forrester could come back, and I could watch the little Scottish lady tie flies at Harkley and Haywood and get my meat from a real butcher shop . . .

(Since writing the above, I've learned that the wonderful compact disc store, the Magic Flute on West 4th Avenue, has closed its doors forever. I want to shout to Chapters, HMV, Sears, and all the big stores, "Goddammit, go away and leave our neighbours alone!")

Heretic Thoughts
on the Typhoon and Stanley Park

In late 2006 a typhoon blew down three-thousand trees in Stanley Park, and great consternation hit the Lower Mainland, hands were wrung, tears flowed while the politicians were ordered to "do something," which usually translates into "hit up the public for some dough." So began fund appeals to "save" Stanley Park.

I have, however, a novel idea: Knock a few more trees down and open up the park so that people can actually walk through the trees. I elevated this trial balloon on my radio show a few years ago and death threats were among the more temperate of responses I got. However, let us face a fact here, folks: This is not old-growth timber we're talking about. That was all chopped down by the beginning of the twentieth century, and a great deal of it stayed chopped, as witness Brockton Point and the land the Aquarium is on.

Let me tell you about my favourite park in the world—Hampstead Heath in London. The distinction between it and Stanley Park is that on Hampstead Heath you don't need a machete to walk amongst the trees. It has a neat combination of wooded areas and open land. It's a place for people and their dogs and is not confined to squirrels and wood bugs.

I love the parks in London. Every time we're there Wendy and I start from Notting Hill and stroll through Kensington Gardens, down to Hyde Park, through there to Green Park and finish with a stroll in St. James's Park to end up at the Cabinet War Rooms and the Churchill Museum. There are lovely fields, copses of plane and oak trees, water features like the Serpentine and Long Water, nannies with babes, dogs unsuccessfully chasing squirrels and, of course, Londoners, eccentric Londoners.

Now, before you unsheathe that assassin's knife, let me say that I know Stanley Park is different. I was born in Vancouver, for God's sake, and know what the park means to a lot of people. All I say is use this opportunity to open up the wooded areas a bit so that people can feel the effect of a woodland—and a very recent woodland at that—not just the appearance of it.

PART XI

Lucky Me!

The Role of Luck

In past books I've spoken about my life at various stages, but now, having exceeded my Biblical span by six years, I want to look back on some of the highlights and the lowlights of my career, though in no particular order. You will see that I've had a goodly share of good fortune, not the least of which was to be born into an upper middle-class family. When asked how I can support some notions of "affirmative action," I reply that it's because I had my own affirmative action in being born where I was and to parents with a "network" which would always assure me of help.

Everyone needs lucky breaks and I've had my share. One night back in early 1975 coming home from Cherry Creek where I had been drinking with business pals, I was more than just impaired at the wheel. I was pissed. I fell asleep at the wheel, crossed the highway, and went down an embankment onto an automobile lot. The RCMP arrived, and for reasons I'll never fathom, the investigating officer asked if I could drive myself home! I nodded my head and drove off, sobered a bit perhaps by the whole affair. I could have killed or maimed someone or several people in addition to killing or maiming myself. If that had happened, quite apart from having to carry that burden forever or simply if I'd been charged with impaired driving or something worse, my political career would have ended before it started, I would never been in the BC cabinet, never gone on radio and never have written eight books.

This event happened at the tail end of the days when impaired driving was still seen as sort of a macho thing. Someone would come into the office on a Monday morning and announce that he had been so "shit-faced" on Saturday night that he had to drive home with one eye closed and the other on the centre line. However, it's no excuse to say that I was no more irresponsible than the average person of that time. I knew better and I recognized that not too big a false step could end my law career much less the political one I was embarking on. After that near-miss I stopped drinking until after the election in December 1975 when I won the Kamloops seat and celebrated with a suds or two. I've given up hard liquor if only because you can never be sure just how much you've had to drink and, in fact, I drank nothing alcoholic at all for nearly thirteen years after my fiftieth birthday.

I have always felt that my behaviour contributed to the death of my seventeen-year-old daughter, Shawn, in 1976. She ran her car into a pole where the road to Cherry Creek and home branches off Highway No. 1. She had been drinking. Might she not have been drinking had I been a better role model? I'll never know, but it's been one of the gremlins I was to combat in later years.

Like most fathers, I daresay, I was close to my daughters. Shawn was a lovely young lady and a very talented one. The blow was immense. Her death contributed to the breakdown of my marriage—a breakdown that was entirely my fault. Eve was able to face Shawn's death better than I could—I needed a shoulder to cry on and unfortunately found one. The tragedy also exposed the fact that Eve and I had grown much apart. I was in politics and doing things I had always wanted to do; Eve loved the home in Cherry Creek, her horses and the country life in general. We had become strangers. Eve, who died in November 2006, never remarried. Another gremlin.

Many a politician has got into trouble for abusing his office, often by throwing his weight about or using official letterhead for private purposes. In early 1976 when I was minister of Consumer Services, I went shopping with my father-in-law-to-be for chemicals for the swimming pool. The salesman charged me sales tax, whereupon Leighton, who had worked in the provincial Ministry of Finance, told the salesman that this stuff was not taxable. In due course the manager came along and after a heated debate supported his sales-man. I very foolishly announced what I did for a living, whereupon the manager started to reverse himself. Suddenly and too late I real-ized I had abused my office. Thankfully the manager didn't make an issue of it after I apologized. He did, however, promise to look into the matter and see if I had a case. I begged him not to, that I would happily pay the tax, but he sent me a cheque a few days later. Had this incident been known to the opposition, I probably would have had to resign.

It got worse. I bought myself a Bulova watch, which continu-ally broke down. I wrote the company—using ministry letterhead, of course—and said, "Your ads say Bulova is guaranteed for life but obviously your definition of 'life' is different from mine." They sent me a new watch. Again, if the opposition had got hold of that one, my career would have ended. I got lucky yet again.

Now one would have thought I had learned my lesson but not so. In late 1976 Eve and I went to Hawaii. This was on our own time and our money. On the way back in first class, we had a simply awful flight. Again I sent a letter, this time to the (now defunct) Western Airlines, on government stationery. Again, rather late in the game, I recognized my error but it was too late. Unannounced, a vice-president of the airlines presented himself at my office to give me a complimentary pair of tick-ets for my trouble. By this time my secretary, Patti (who would later be my wife), seeing the jam I was in, carefully and skillfully extracted me from it. By this time I think I got the hang of it and made no more errors like that! In sum, without the greatest of luck and forebearance of others I would have had my political career in tatters before I started or in ruins shortly afterwards.

I had an earlier stroke of good luck without which I wouldn't have got into law school. I had flunked second-year Arts—it hadn't helped that I hadn't bothered to write the exams—and I only went back for another try through the extreme patience and support of my parents. When I got to the end of third-year Arts—which I completed with a second class average—I still had not passed French 202, a condition for entering law school, though I had now taken it three times! The French 202 exam traditionally emphasized the book that the class had read and since I didn't even know what the book was—not having attended any lectures—I was getting ready to go to summer school. On the day of the exam a girlfriend asked why I wasn't studying for my French exam. I told her that not only had I not read the prescribed book, but I didn't even know its name.

My friend Molly Lou Shaw (who would be my sister-in-law for over twenty years) said, "It's St-Exupery's *Vol de Nuit*," and offered me the English translation, *Night Flight*. It's a short book so I took it down to the Main Library and read it. When exam time came, I thought, what the hell? Maybe I can fake it and what is there to lose? To my unbelieving eyes the first question, worth 75 out 150 marks, asked for a précis of *Vol de Nuit* in *English!* I received 76 out of 150 and I was off to law school.

I did decently enough in law school, graduating in the top one-third, but by the time I graduated Eve and I had a baby son and there was no way I could afford to article at $150 per month, so I took a job with Imperial Oil in Edmonton. I hated Edmonton so a few months later came back to Vancouver and went to work for a MacMillan Bloedel subsidiary, Canadian White Pine, as a junior safety supervisor. I hated the place and after perhaps four weeks I ran into a buddy from law school, Roy Logie, who was working as a claims adjustor at Allstate Insurance (wryly referred to as "All Heart Insurance" in light of their stinginess and a habit of cancelling the policy of anyone who had an accident). I went to see Allstate and was hired starting in one week's time. The following morning—I had been told it was coming—the manager of Canadian White Pine, Ed McDonald, fired me, giving two weeks' notice. Since my pay at Allstate was to be the same as at CWP ($350 per month), I got an extra week's pay, which, considering my financial condition, was little short of a miracle! I hated Allstate, too. The main command there was to "control" the injured party, which meant keeping them away from lawyers. This meant being very economical with the truth, such as telling them that Allstate would pay them more net than any lawyer could get them after his fees were paid.

I still badly wanted to article and get back into law, but I just couldn't do it on the pittance that law firms paid articled students. Then a double dose of good luck came my way. I was a pretty fair golfer and I learned that the teaching pro at Golflands Driving Range, near the airport, had quit. Over a beer at the local beer parlour (starting a tradition, I might add) I asked the owner, the late Al Gleeson, if I could be his new teaching professional, and he hired me. I was to get $3.50 for each half-hour lesson and on a weekend could sometimes earn over $40—big money in 1960. With this new-found wealth I went looking for a spot to article since the going rate for articles and what I made teaching golf would actually bring in a little more money than I was making at Allstate. I applied at the old and distinguished firm of Guild Yule and Company, and Mr. Yule hired me at $250 per month. Then I ran into one of my former colleagues at Allstate, Al Helgason, who was just finishing his articles with Thomas (Tommy) Griffiths, the famous damages lawyer who pioneered the use of the civil jury in damage actions in British Columbia. Al suggested I talk to Tommy who paid well if students knew anything about damages law, and to cut to the chase, I accepted an offer of $150 a *week* that was to go up to $175 after six months. I then went down the one floor that separated Tommy Griffiths' offices from those of Messrs. Guild Yule and Co. to un-hire myself. Ken Yule, QC, was livid. He acted for many insurance companies, and in his view Tommy, by racking up big jury awards, was nothing but a shyster. Ken all but threw me out of his office. (Later we made up and became friends.)

Now with $150 per week coming from articles and as much as $100 or more from teaching fees, by the standards of the day I was doing very well indeed! A lucky hiring, a lucky firing, a lucky opening at a golf range and a lucky articling job and all of a sudden Eve and I were doing just fine.

Going on to more mundane matters, in 1984 I went broke. I had worked for CJOR 600AM for about forty months when, after horrendous negotiations with the manager, I was fired. I'd had the feeling that my wife and I were in a bit of financial trouble, but I had no idea how bad it was. By any definition I was certainly bankrupt, being a net $250,000 in the hole with the tax department, one of my principal creditors. For one thing, my house was worth less than the mortgages—plural. I remember one hot day that summer I received a notice of foreclosure on the house and a vicious call from the tax department, whereupon I went out into the pool, lay back on a rubber raft and told myself that I'd better enjoy this while I could.

Then I got another double dose of good luck. I had sued Jimmy Pattison on the basis that his manager had negotiated in bad faith. Evidently Jimmy agreed and he paid me nearly $50,000 by way of settlement, and this went to the tax department and calmed them down for a bit. Then we had a visit from our good friends Dick and Joanna Lillico who were also special good friends of Grace and Ray McCarthy and they invited Patti and me to a cocktail party in the Lillicos' honour. There I ran into John Plul who was CKNW's PR man. I didn't know John well except by reputation: He was the public relations man nonpareil. When he asked me what I was doing, I told him that I was looking for work, and though I did have a job offer from

Campney Murphy to go back into the practise of law, I really wanted to broadcast. John asked me to drop in to CKNW at nine on Monday morning so we could chat some more. I did so and was surprised — nay, shocked — to see all of the "brass" there and our "chat" being chaired by Ted Smith, the general manager. To my huge surprise I was offered a job as host of a new midnight-to-two a.m. talk show to be called *Nightline BC*. I couldn't accept fast enough! The money was no hell and I had to provide my own producer, who happened to be Patti and who, incidentally, became a top-notch producer.

After a year CKNW offered me an evening talk show and after a year of that, Lady Luck struck again! I had just arrived at a London flat I was using for a side business that I was involved in when Patti phoned to say that Barrie Clark, the well-known afternoon host, was leaving. Since the program manager, Doug Rutherford, had always told me I was next in line, I was looking forward to talking to him. But when I phoned him, he wasn't quite so positive. No matter. In due course the good luck became fact, and within two years I had moved from undeclared bankruptcy to the number-two talk-show host in the province. CKNW did not pay me any more, as they had promised, but less than two years later Gary Bannerman, the number-one host, left and again, after some futzing about during which time Jack Webster filled in, I was named Gary's successor. In less than four years I'd gone from undeclared bankruptcy to number-one talk-show host in the province — and some say the country. Pretty good luck, I would say! It's true that I had proved myself, but any time someone moves into a new time slot it's a gamble. And I had no right or reason to believe that the two hosts ahead of me, both of whom were younger, would leave openings for me. If someone had said in 1984 that in less than four years the relatively young number-one and number-two men would leave CKNW and that I would be the "top dog," I would have pronounced them mad!

My next bit of good luck came in 1990. I had been a fishing pal of Fin Anthony's for some years — in fact, virtually every week we fly-fished the beaches of the Sunshine Coast for sea-run cutthroat. Fin had spent a long career in advertising and knew the media inside out. Over the time we fished Fin had become aware that I was very unhappy with the way 'NW was holding my salary down. He knew as I did that they could do this for two reasons: There was no talk show competing with us to give me any leverage at contract time plus the management knew the terrible financial shape I was in. Business comes a long way before compassion in the media game. We did no more than talk about any of this until one day— and I can't recall who raised the idea—Fin agreed to be my agent. He instantly promised that, although I was in the middle of a three-year contract, he would get me a $50,000 signing bonus on a new contract worth double what I was getting.

"How?" I asked.

"Well," Fin replied, "having read your contract, I note that you are not bound to give an editorial off the top and that's what sets up the show. We just hint—and if necessary belt them with the idea–that we might just 'work to rule.' In other words, no fair contract no more editorial."

It was brilliant and within a month I had a new contract that gave me more than double what I had been making plus a signing bonus, though it was "only" $40,000! We had a big party at a posh downtown hotel and Premier Mike Harcourt even attended! I should have thought of having Fin as my agent long before. He went on to get me a short-term but profitable TV contract with KVOS and some nice writing jobs, and I believe he negotiated one more contract with 'NW for me before we split.

The reason we split was sad and personal. Though we're no longer even friends, I have to say that financially Fin Anthony was the best thing to happen for me in many a moon, though, as you will see, meeting Wendy was even better—and not only because she knew how to handle money. I will always be grateful and sorry that my friendship with Fin ended.

In 1993 the luckiest thing of my life happened: I met Wendy. I've told the story elsewhere, but suffice it to say that I was to lead a tour of the UK and Ireland and, being in the UK ahead of the gang, I went out to Heathrow to meet them. I saw this lovely lady coming towards me and was almost knocked off my feet. To cut to the chase, four days later when we were in Exeter I asked her to marry me and she agreed. I went back to Vancouver ten days before she did and, although I had promised to phone her a few days after I got back, I phoned her every day and sometimes several times a day. When she arrived back on September 7, 1993, I moved into her apartment with my thirteen garbage bags full of clothes plus a computer, and as soon as we each were rid of legal impedimenta, we married. On July 29, 2008, will be fourtenn years married and in September fifteen years together. Wendy has turned my life around in every way. She gave me the fiscal management I'd never had before and became an instant grandmother to my then seven, now eight, grandchildren. She had another lover, however—my then five-year-old chocolate Labrador, Clancy. He, like his master, fell instantly in love with Wendy and she with him. Mostly, Wendy gave me love.

I had more good luck to come. In June 2003 CKNW spent four months trying to get me to quit. In July 2002 I had signed a new three-year contract with them for about $330,000 per annum, and whether the people at Corus thought they had paid too much I'll never know. Do I think it was advertiser pressure? Of course I do, but that scarcely makes it so. It started as a concentrated hassle over how I had treated an employee—one of my sins was "demanding" that my producer put the sprinkles in my coffee at Starbucks!—but it was nevertheless very sad. I loved my days with 'NW. I covered a hell of a lot of issues—Meech Lake/Charlottetown, the Kemano II project, gravel pits, fish farms, and the one I relate to most, mental health. Moreover, I was flying. I had never felt better or so full of piss and vinegar. But all good things come to an end. I just wish that CKNW could have shown some class towards a broadcaster who for nineteen years was number one in his time slot.

The good luck?

They had to pay me for a year and since I joined AM600 I had a year of nearly double pay.

Changes Along the Way

After a lifetime of doing it I've stopped fishing. I was into catch-and-release, of course, long before I quit, but when it dawned on me that I was tormenting animals for pleasure, it just wasn't fun any more. (See *Over the Mountains* for the full story.) I've never been much for hunting though I know it's illogical to fish for pleasure and not shoot for pleasure. I killed a squirrel with a .22 when I was a boy and have etched in my mind that little dead animal at my feet, tiny testicles up (his, not mine), with me asking why did you do that, Rafe?

I'm opposed to seal hunts and whale hunts. Not only are they unethical, or ought to be, but they are totally unnecessary. We're told by the Newfie sealers that it's their way of life, that they just love killing baby seals every year and the government obliges them, subsidizing them, even making it against the law to take pictures of their horrible pastime. I cannot believe that as a Canadian taxpayer my taxes are being used to subsidize this repulsive slaughter and also to bring to "justice" any who photograph and report on this terrible blot on the national escutcheon.

In my dotage I've become much more enraged at government arrogance than I was. When I see federal and provincial departments getting together not to enforce the law but to shill for Atlantic-salmon fish farmers, I get very cross. When I listen to their lies, I have no tolerance left. And when I see governments make huge, environmentally sensitive decisions on schemes like the Gateway Project and then do the environmental assessment *after* the decision has been made, I lose all sense of humour.

Although I don't believe I've shifted my political position much over the years, I must admit that I am finding some of the positions taken by the left appealing. But those who think I've only lately become a "leftie" forget that my first act when I became Consumer Services minister in 1975 was to bring in legislation to get rid of the leeches in the beer parlours who were buying tax rebates at a huge rip-off discount. I don't believe in the theory that has tax reductions for the rich dripping down to the poor. That doesn't happen. I don't believe that a rising tide lifts all boats because, if your anchor is too heavy, you'll drown and figuratively that's what happens to the poor.

Certainly I'm a conservative in the sense that I'm an environmentalist but I've always been that. However, though I'm certainly not a socialist nor close to joining the NDP, I would feel more comfortable being in a Carole James government than one led by Gordon Campbell.

On Cruising

I came late to cruising because I was certain that there would be a man in a white uniform on board trying to get me to play some damned game or guess when we would cross the equator. The mental image of this nuisance-in-uniform completely obliterated any thoughts of having a good time.

My first cruise was in 1990 down the Nile but it really didn't count because it was just a little thing of a boat. The first big one was on the Princess Lines from Athens through the Mediterranean to Dover in 1997. I think I had a good time though mostly I just remember having my doubts about cruising dashed. We next took a trip to Tahiti where we boarded the *Windstar*, a "computerized sailboat," to tour the islands. The sails are mostly for show but the trip was simply great. We then took a trip starting in Fort Lauderdale, Florida, through the Panama Canal and down the west coast of South America to Valparaiso/Santiago. This was getting to be fun! Since then we've done the Baltic, the eastern Mediterranean, the east coast of South America from Buenos Aires and round the Horn to Valparaiso/Santiago, and a double cruise of the Caribbean. I have become addicted such that at the end of November 2006 we went to Rome and took a "repositioning" cruise that ended in New Orleans— or what's left of it. A repositioning cruise is when they move a vessel, because of the season change, from one run to another, and they are about half-price. These cruises are a bargain, but remember you're travelling in the off season, not the hot one.

Then in June 2007 we booked on another Windstar from Rome to Venice via the Dalmatian Coast. It was only seven days but gave us a wonderful look at this part of the world. The highlights were Dubrovnik in Croatia and the entrance via the Grand Canal to Venice. In November 2007 we sailed on Holland America from Lisbon to South America via Cadiz in Spain, Casablanca in Morocco and Dakar in Senegal to Recife and Salvador in Brazil, finishing with three days in Rio de Janeiro.

But isn't cruising expensive? It depends. If you were to add up the gas, the meals and the hotels of a motor vacation, a cruise comes off very well, bearing in mind that the travel, room and board on a cruise has been prepaid and you only have to unpack and pack twice. Where you stay on board makes a big difference; if you don't have a porthole, it's much cheaper. Shore excursions can be expensive and I advise that you look at these carefully, and bear in mind that, if you are docking in a city, four sharing a taxi will cost perhaps $50 per couple and you'll see and learn more. So there we are—the old grouch tried cruising and loves it.

The Play's the Thing

Sometimes you simply have to walk away and say to hell with it. Day after bloody day of wars, desecration of the environment, drive-by shootings and the lot makes one insensitive if a fresh inhalation of oxygen isn't taken. With that in mind, let's go to London where there are always places to get full mental relief—the theatres. In 2006, a stressful year for me, I went to four musicals there that I want to tell you about just in case you may be going soon to Blighty, since at this writing they're all still playing. Please note that these are not the only ones; you will always find many more that are both interesting and a distraction from the horrors of the daily fare the media dishes out.

Mamma Mia, which Wendy and I have seen four times, is a must, especially if you're an ABBA fan, and who isn't? The plot concerns a young woman on the eve of her marriage, who wants to invite her father to the wedding but doesn't know who he is and her mother won't tell. The young bride-to-be gets a hold of Mom's diary and discovers that there are three possibilities so she invites all three. It's a wonderful, fun-filled musical.

Andrew Lloyd Webber has brought *Evita* back. It is my favourite of all his efforts and when Wendy and I saw it, far from being disappointed as so often happens with a revival, we were, in fact, overwhelmed by the production and all the familiar music.

Last year Lloyd Webber, acting as producer, also brought *Mary Poppins* to the stage and it is a blockbuster success with Laura Michelle Kelly playing a marvelous Mary. It got one of those rare — in London — spontaneous standing ovations.

But I've saved the best for last. Last year we went to the revival of *Sound of Music*, again produced by Andrew Lloyd Webber. It simply blew us away as we heard the songs we know so well replayed with such talent. Lloyd Webber needed a fresh star for the role of Maria so used a BBC1 show called *How Do We Fix A Problem Like Maria?* to find her. The role was won by a hitherto unknown performer, Connie Fisher, who is no longer unknown as she has played Maria to the point where even hardened old cynical reviewers are singing her praises.

Now just to clear up any misapprehensions you may have, Lord Lloyd Webber did not write the music for *Mary Poppins* or *The Sound of Music*. They contain all the same music we loved so well when they were first produced: The Sherman brothers' songs for *Mary Poppins* and the Rodgers and Hammerstein score for *The Sound of Music*.

So there we are. Just for a moment we sit back, fold our newspapers, turn off our radios and TVs, say to hell with our cells and blackberries and take ourselves to faraway places, transplanting ourselves, mentally if not physically, to a place where there is still amusement that doesn't have blood, gore and "modern sex." I know that most don't have the ability to hop the pond to take in the theatre, but we all can dream and hope despite the sad state of affairs into which our world has descended.

And who knows? Sometimes dreams come true.

Not for the Faint of Heart #2

In my last book, *Over the Mountains,* I did a chapter on growing old and, although I'm now a year older, I thought it had said it all. It hadn't.

You are only young once, they tell me. Old age is not for the faint of heart. The hardest part is going to class reunions and reading the obituary pages. At the fiftieth anniversary of our UBC law class those who were there seemed so much older than I, and they remembered the damndest things, things I'd have sooner left in the murky recesses of aging minds. And when I get past a weekend with only one or two familiar names on the obituary page, I feel lucky. Often it's someone I've forgotten, such as a guy who I used to sing with in the boys' choir at St. Mary's church. Ken Gunning was the head guy who got to carry the big brass cross and who died in April of 2007. And I ask myself, is it possible that they're going to make an exception in my case?

Another of the hard parts of growing old is that, when I go for old-age perks such as ferry rides, no one has ever asked me to prove my age! And then there's having people do things for me such as pick up things I've dropped and always opening the bloody door for me.

There are compensations, of course. I have two knees that are bone-on-bone so use a walking stick (I refuse to call it a cane), which means on the London Underground someone always gives me a seat.

I don't much like reminiscing—at least not for too long. Being young before rock and roll has left my generation with a lot of music memories to add a big dose of bitter-sweet to the days that pass so quickly. But sometimes a small surprise gives that same sort of bitter-sweet feeling, too. The other day my email brought a promotion for a new book on the history of the Dunbar neighbourhood of Vancouver. I went to school at St. George's in Dunbar during World War II and there was a picture on the book's cover, taken at that time in front of the Dunbar Theatre with a streetcar number seven in front of it. I thought about the movies we used to go to there at ten cents for a kid and that number seven streetcar. Good old number seven. Then, the same day, I saw a bus with Dunbar on the marquee and it was number seven. Just a tiny bit of nostalgia but kind of neat.

I've never had a long attention span but now, more than ever, I tire easily of listening about aches, pains and death. In fact, we and a couple we often dine with have a ten-minute rule: After ten minutes of blood, strange operations, death and disability the conversation must change. It's a good rule. And my time for plays, movies, concerts and the like is two hours max. I went to an opera that was four hours long and I felt like a wild animal in a cage. Two hours is plenty.

The other day I read a story about an *elderly* couple, aged sixty-seven and sixty-three respectively, et cetera, et cetera. Elderly? In one's sixties? Who writes this garbage? Who edits it? Of course, they say that death is a good thing and that, if we've behaved ourselves, we'll go to eternal paradise, but if that's so, why do popes hang on to the very last thread of life? After all, aren't they high up on the "A" list? Some say no one wants to live to be a hundred, but tell that to someone who is ninety-nine! And how come no one knows what "heaven" is? As D.P. Barron once said, "Millions long for immortality who don't know what to do with themselves on a rainy Sunday afternoon."

On December 31, 2006, while I was helping out on the New Year's Eve champagne bar at Jurys Hotel in South Kensington, I asked myself over and over, "Mair, how the hell did you ever get to be seventy-five, considering some of the lifestyles you've had?" I don't know the answer, but I do know that when my time comes, I'll fight every bit as hard as any pope ever did!

The Other Side

I have had three examples of another world at work so that I believe that there is something beyond the scene in which we all are born and all will die.

In October 1976 my seventeen-year-old daughter was killed in a car accident. A few weeks later Greg, one of her circle of friends, came to me to ask if I minded if he told me something about Shawn. "Of course not," I replied, and he told me that, after she had died, Shawn spoke to him and said, "Please tell my mom and dad that I'm sorry but that I am happy." Needless to say, it shook me and I thanked Greg for talking with me.

Some months later I became aware that a woman had been trying to speak to me. I was an MLA at the time and my staff kept her away because they thought she was a troublesome kook. I asked to see the woman. She said, "I am psychic, and although your daughter didn't know me, she spoke to me after she was killed and said, "Tell my mom and dad that I'm sorry but that I'm happy." There is no way this woman, who lived in Heffley Creek, would have known Greg.

In 1993 I fell head over heels in love with Wendy. I was sitting in my office at the CKNW Expo site preparing to go on air. Suddenly Wendy appeared beside me for a few seconds and then left. It didn't scare me or even startle me—it just happened.

In 2006, a couple of hours after we had gone to bed, I woke to see a woman coming through the bedroom door. I had no feeling of fear nor was I really startled. As I went for the light, I asked her who she was and what she wanted. She stared at me then slowly dissolved.

When Wendy told Trudy, who has lived in a nearby townhouse for many years, about this event, Trudy asked Wendy to have me describe this apparition. I recalled her as being forty-ish, stout though not really fat, and wearing a strange white hat. Trudy told us that many years earlier a woman had committed suicide in the bathroom right beside our bedroom. She showed me a picture of about ten women at a party, none of whom I knew and I picked her out immediately. No doubt in the world. But what about her unusual white hat? Then it dawned on me she had been a nurse and practised in the days when nurses still wore the caps from the hospital where they had trained.

I have no doubt that there is something beyond this vale of tears though I haven't the faintest idea of what that might be.

Don Quixote at Peace

For too many years I have tilted at windmills. It's hard work and it's the kind of work you can never really abandon for more than an hour or so. And I love it. I'm one of those people lucky enough to have his hobby his profession. But still, there has to be more to life than just work and vacations accompanied by a laptop.

So I have a time—about an hour a day—that acts as a cleansing agent for the brain.

As my readers know, we have a wonderful chocolate Labrador called Chauncey. When we first got him at about eight weeks, we took him down to one of the beaches near our home in Lions Bay. "Surely," Wendy said, "it's too cold in January to send him into that water!" "Let's let him make that decision," I replied as I tossed a stick about twenty feet into the water. Chauncey charged in after it but when his little feet couldn't touch the bottom any more, he looked back at us as if to say "What now?" Then he turned back to get the stick, brought it in and dropped it at my feet as he wagged his tail for more. He hasn't missed a day since, no matter what the season or weather. From early on he has chased a tennis ball thrown out by use of a sling so his swims are pretty long ones.

We call the beach we go to Bow Wow Beach since that's where the Lions Bay canines come to swim and it is truly a wondrous place. Wendy and I sit on a log and can see Horseshoe Bay to our left and out to Bowyer Island on our right. Across the way is Hood Point on Bowen Island where I spent some very happy hours with my friends, the Shields, so many years ago. We look up Collingwood Channel between Bowen and Gambier Island, another of my boyhood stomping grounds.

Almost every day we have a curious seal come up to see what's going on. In April last, one morning we had seven seals watching Chauncey swim for his tennis ball. They are amazing animals, seldom in evidence when we arrive, but once Chauncey starts his swims it seems that the seals' curiosity is aroused and they pop up all over. Many times we've had one or two seals surface right alongside him—indeed, one stole his tennis ball from right under his nose! The fact that he takes no notice tells me he knows they mean him no harm. We also have a family of sea otters nearby and they will often swim in quite close and do the sort of acrobatics for which they're so famous. We have eagles, both bald and golden, and spotting them in a tree or seeing them in their graceful flight across, I suppose, to Bowen Island is a sight one never tires of.

Bow Wow Beach is almost a private club. There are, perhaps, a half dozen other dogs that are brought down for a visit and perhaps a swim. We are a special band, we think, and look over any newcomer with some suspicion. (In reality, we get to know the names and personalities of the dogs before we get to know their masters/mistresses.) On the other hand, if I don't see Elizabeth and her wonderful spaniel, Amy Jane, I worry. I hope nothing's happened!

One morning last winter while taking Chauncey for his daily swim, it occurred to me that maybe I should talk about the forthcoming provincial budget in my online column for *The Tyee*. But the thought quickly passed and I mumbled, "To hell with it." Anyway, it's always the same, somehow. I could write the NDP and Liberal responses to the budget and those of business and labour long before the minister makes his/her speech. Same old, same old. But as I sat on a log waiting for the world's greatest retriever to return from the briny with his tennis ball, I saw something I hadn't seen for a long, long time in our waters—a big commercial troller. We don't see them anymore. Why would we? There's nothing left to troll for. And it took me back to my childhood at Granthams Landing where my grandfather had a cottage. Actually it was a shack . . . well, no, it wasn't even that luxurious. In the morning I would watch all the trollers, in single file, motor out of Gibson's Landing heading towards Gower Point, the two Popham Islands and other productive spots. My dad and mom and I would often go out there, too, trolling Tom Mack spoons, and I would listen to the bells at the end of the trollers' long, angular, upright sticks and wait for the bell to go nuts, meaning there was a fish on.

I remember the men with herring rakes, stout poles with sharp metal nails in them, sweeping them through the ubiquitous schools of herring and throwing their catch into their live bait buckets. No one rakes herring schools any more; there aren't many herring left and, besides, what would you use them as bait for?

I remember as a university student working out in Steveston at BC Packers and using a pole with a spike on it (called a pew) to unload thousands of pinks, sockeye and coho. It was hard work in the hot sun but you saw what your province was all about: Wild salmon. (I had my moment of fame when the company's PR man brought some guests to see the 100-pound Chinook we had. A co-worker and I took hold of this denizen of the deep, but it slipped out of our hands and into the murky Fraser River. We were not popular.) But the Steveston BC Packers is gone, too.

So when a BC Environment minister or a federal Fisheries minister holds a press conference to tell us that the salmon, herring, fishboats and herring rakes are back, then maybe I'll listen to what a member of the government has to say. I'm not holding my breath until that happens.

Now as we look out, Wendy and I often wonder out loud why we spend all that money going to faraway places when they have little if anything that can match this! On the fine days, it's a beautiful and colourful sight to behold. When it's dull or raining, it becomes a symphony of blacks, whites and silvers, a rare beauty all its own. So life in the fast lane tilting at windmills has, for me, a nearby slow lane: Bow Wow Beach.

Index